Shannon

Separating Fact from Fiction: The Life of a Consensual Slave in the 21st Century

DV8 Books

DV8 Publishing

http://dv8publishing.com

i

All DV8 titles, imprints and distributed lines are available at special quantity discounts for bulk purchases for sales promotions, premiums, fund raising, educational or institutional use.

Special book excerpts or customized printings can also be created to fit specific needs. For details, write or phone the office of the DV8 Special Sales Manager, DV8 Publishing, 2525 McNeill Circle, Fayetteville, NC 28303, Attn: Special Sales Department.

ISBN: **9781440473630**

First DV8 Trade Paperback Printing: January 2008

Printed in the United States of America

Perhaps you've picked up this book because you are considering a consensual slavery relationship. Maybe you're already engaged in such a relationship and you're looking for voices like yours. Whatever your reason for choosing this book, thank you.

In this book you'll find frank discussion of the realities of creating and living a life of consensual slavery. I've included experiences and anecdotes from my own life so you'll know you're not alone. I've also presented some practical approaches to creating and sustaining a consensual slavery relationship which I hope you'll find helpful.

In the end, the relationship you engage in will be entirely different from mine. While I recognize that interpersonal relationships are unique, I hope that you'll find enough of what you need in this book to help you decide if consensual slavery is good for you or not. Consensual slavery isn't easy, but it can be wonderful and fulfilling if you're willing to work at it.

Thank you, once again, for choosing this book, and I hope you enjoy this part of your journey.

Shannon Reilly

I am many things in this life: woman, teacher, lover, slave. Each day I live all of these roles and do so joyfully, studiously, and judiciously. Sometimes they conflict, hence the use of a pen name for this book, and sometimes they are so close to each other there is no room for differentiation.

I've been a member of the Leather lifestyle and community [1]since 2001 and have grown immensely in the time I have spent here. I've lived a 24/7 consensual slavery life and I've run lifestyle businesses. I've supported the community and cursed it as well. In short, I've been human.

By day, I teach English at a community college. By night I write, I crochet, and I make whips (when my hands don't hurt too much). I read everything I can and have reveled in the literature of our community since it was a lifeline to others when I was alone.

This book has been a labor of love for me. As a consensual slave, I know how hard it can be to search the contemporary leather literature for voices like mine and to find them lacking or too impersonal. I have looked for voices like mine and when I didn't find them in our books, I decided to share mine.

I hope you enjoy the book. Please do feel free to contact me at shannon@dv8publishing.com if you have questions or comments. I look forward to hearing from you.

---

[1] To me, the Leather Community includes not only the play of BDSM activities but also the structure of power exchange relationships. I have found that the communities which I include in my definition of the Leather Community often separate themselves based on their preferences and activities, but I prefer to keep them together based on their similarities.

Acknowledgements

I have many people to thank for their help, support and input on this book.

First, the man I serve. Thank you for your support and conviction that I could do this. Your support keeps me going every time I falter.

Next, my dear friend Rick. You comforted me when I cried and listened to me kvetch as I lived the experiences that became this book. You were always just a phone call or instant message away and you even suffered through reading the first draft. Thank you, my friend.

Mr. D., you've unfailingly been there when I needed a shoulder to cry on. You never stinted on yourself and your availability and I treasure your friendship.

Jack Rinella, I want to thank you for the kick in the ass you delivered while seated on the couch at the club in October 2007. Your point that we weren't writing enough as a community was well taken and I hope you are proud of this book as you were the inspiration for me to begin writing again.

Viola Johnson, you've always been there when I needed to ask a question. Your book has always been a source of comfort and awe for me. I hope you enjoy this book and I thank you for everything you've done for the leather community.

To my readers, thank you for your comments and input. Your help has made this book better with each draft.

To everyone I've ever bounced ideas off of, eavesdropped on conversations with, or flat out cornered for an opinion, thank you. Your time and input are apparent in every word I've written for this book. The community has been instrumental in the path I've taken to find my place as a consensual slave in the 21st century. I only hope that those who read this book can benefit as much from your wisdom as I have.

The Humble Monk Page

In order to avoid the repetition of the "humble monk" phrases so often found in contemporary non-fiction texts, I want to include a single, all-encompassing one here.

The definitions, opinions, concepts and suggestions found in this text represent the collective knowledge and experiences of the author. I understand that your experiences and opinions may vary drastically from mine and I hope you are willing to set aside those differences while you read this book. I will not apologize for my views, but will make every effort to present them respectfully.

For the purpose of clarity and avoiding cumbersome textual conventions, the author has used the following terms interchangeably:

- dominant, master, mistress, owner, top
- slave, servant, submissive, bottom
- Leather Community, BDSM, WIITWD (What it is that we do)

The relationships described herein often mirror those the author has engaged in; specifically a male owner and a female servant dynamic. While I cannot write of experiences I haven't lived, there should be no reason why you cannot interchange pronouns and genders to match your experiences and preferences.

Additionally, since the author is an English teacher, proper grammatical conventions for capitalization will be maintained throughout this text. Please do not take offense to the refusal to randomly capitalize role designators such as master or top. Rather rejoice in the presentation of information in a manner which abides by the rules of Standard American English.

A Note to and About Switches

You will note that there is no mention of switches[2] in this book other than in the glossary. There is a reason for that. I am not a switch and so I cannot speak about the experiences of a switch.

That being said, I hope if you are a switch, you will still find value in the ideas presented in this book. As a switch you have the luxury of reading this book from both the dominant and submissive perspective. I hope that you'll take from it those things you find applicable to your life, regardless of the role you most closely identify with.

Please know that I have not forgotten the role switches play in the leather community. But since I don't know enough about the switch perspective, I would not do it justice to attempt to present it here.

---

[2] A person in the Leather Community who alternately identifies as both top and bottom or both master and slave

Table of Contents

Definitions and Discussions

It is critical that we are on the same page when it comes to definitions if we are going to make progress toward understanding. Members of the Leather Community often have differing definitions for similar terms, necessitating a clear definition prior to discussion of the term. This first section tackles that issue by defining and discussing important ideas, concepts, and issues for the consensual slave. Please understand that I am not presenting my definitions as the one and only possibility. Rather I am giving you my viewpoint so we can begin our journey on the same road.

What is Consensual Slavery?

As someone who has spent the better part of her adult life working with the English language, I recognize the contradiction in the term "consensual slave." However, despite that contradiction, consensual slavery can be a way of life.

For me, the term "slave" conjures two types of images. First, I might picture the naked black man or woman chained to the wall in the hold of a ship as the white slavers threaten them with galley whips and other violence. This image usually includes tears and resignation in the eyes of these obviously captured men and woman. Or perhaps I've read too many erotic novels and I envision some beautiful man or woman artfully displayed in a dungeon or sitting room while masters and mistresses[3] erotically torture the supplicant. The truth of the matter is that in the 21st century, a slave might be the woman in the next office, the man who signs your paychecks, or the couple who lives next door. Consensual slavery is not only for the novels of *The Marketplace* [4]series, but a way of life for many men and women.

The key differences between the slaves of the past and those of the contemporary Leather or BDSM[5] lifestyle are consent and free will. Twenty-first century slaves are consenting adults who freely choose to offer their service to other consenting adults for various reasons. Contemporary consensual slavery is an activity between adults and should contain no elements of coercion (prior to the conclusion of relationship negotiations, of course). Additionally, consensual slavery or servitude creates a relationship in which either party can withdraw consent at any time.

The myth that the slave is really in control of the relationship is perpetuated by those who believe only the servant's role requires consent.

---

[3] An honorific used to identify the dominant member of a power exchange relationship.
[4] *The Marketplace* is the first in a series of books by Laura Antoniou. For me, it was the first fiction that actually addressed what a life of consensual slavery could be like if an organization like The Marketplace existed for training and placing consensual slaves.
[5] Acronym for various permutations of Bondage/Discipline, Dominance/Submission, Sadism/Masochism. Used as a broad term to define the activities practiced in relationships of this type.

The truth is, without someone consenting to accept your service, and continuing to consent, you cannot serve as a consensual slave. I find it interesting to watch interactions and listen to discussions in the community on the topic of consent. So often only the submissive's consent is considered, when the reality is that both members of a power exchange[6] relationship must first give and then continue to give their consent in order to form a successful relationship.

There have been times as I've observed interactions between submissives and dominants when it has become obvious there is a misconception that a dominant need not give consent for activities. I've watched submissives drape themselves on dominants without any concern for their comfort or consent. Often these situations are laughed off in spite of any discomfort the dominant might feel. Now reverse the roles. What do you call the dominant who touches without asking first? Why the double standard? We're adults engaged in adult activities. We must take responsibility for our actions and ensure that consent is given by all involved before any activity is undertaken. It is important to remember that without the consent of all parties, there is no relationship.

I define a total power exchange relationship (i.e. a consensual slavery relationship) as a relationship between equals that is not egalitarian. The owner[7] and the slave are equals in this type of relationship, even if the workload isn't "fair.". If you've observed a consensual slavery relationship from the outside, you have likely noticed the apparent disparity in what the day to day tasks of the owner and slave might be. And if you've lived a consensual slavery relationship, you know that often there is disparity in the workload, but that the relationship work [8]is actually equally distributed. It's true that I might have the tasks of cleaning the bathroom and kitchen while the owner doesn't engage in such activities, but the hard work of the relationship, the communication, connection and negotiation, are equally distributed between us.

---

[6] The giving and receiving of power in a sadomasochistic relationship.
[7] A gender non-specific honorific used to identify the dominant member of a power exchange relationship. This term is used in this text to identify the dominant members of total power exchange relationships.
[8] Relationship work is everything parties must do to keep the relationship healthy. Keeping lines of communication open and clear, maintaining connection and continuing to meet the needs of your partners are just some of the aspects of relationship work.

In any relationship, failure on the part of one of the members to work at the relationship will likely result in the failure of the relationship. Such is doubly true in consensual slavery relationships where the owner holds the responsibility of creating an environment in which the servant can be successful while at the same time the servant carries the responsibility of maintaining an environment in which the owner can be successful. Yes, the owner can override the wants and desires of the servant, and often will. This arrangement is what often gives the appearance of an unfair distribution of labor. But if the negotiations of the relationship were comprehensive and the expectations of the relationship are being upheld, the servant and owner remain equals and maintain equal responsibility for the success of the relationship.

It is a refrain you will hear from me again and again in this book, these relationships are for and by adults. Adults can and must take responsibility for their actions. If you do not feel as though you are equal to the one you wish to serve, consider why you want to enter into consensual slavery. If you are looking solely for someone to take care of you and remove your need to be a responsible adult, likely consensual slavery is not for you.

As equals, the members of a consensual slavery relationship will exchange power with each other, giving and taking that power in a constant flow. Power is neither created nor destroyed in power exchange relationships. Rather two equals remain equal while power flows between them. Think of it in terms of the Lomonosov-Lavoisier law of the conservation of matter.

The Lomonosov-Lavoisier law states, "the mass of a closed system will remain constant, regardless of the processes acting inside the system" (Conservation of matter, 2007). If we envision a power exchange relationship as a closed system, i.e. one in which two or more consenting adults join together, each bringing an equal amount of responsibility (power) for the relationship to the table, then it becomes clear that regardless of protocol, etiquette, or day-to-day tasks (the processes of a power exchange relationship) the volume of power in the relationship does not change. The owner and the slave remain equals.

The exchange of power in a consensual slavery relationship is much more akin to the rolling waves of an ocean than to the stacking of weights on a balance or scale, hence my statement that they are not egalitarian. No matter how big the swell of the wave, there is an accompanying dip in the ocean, and the two together encompass an unchanging volume of water. With each act of submission, the slave offers the master a portion of his or her power. By accepting the submission, the owner offers a portion of his or her power via trust that tasks will be completed. Power may ebb and flow between partners in a power exchange but power is neither created nor destroyed in this process. In the end, the equals who entered the relationship remain equals for the duration.

BDSM activities are best suited to responsible adults who are willing to accept responsibility for and the consequences of their actions. The myth of the enslaved woman who cannot leave the tyrannical master because he won't "release" her is ridiculous. The master and slave in this myth are both supposedly adults. The slave has a brain, a mouth and two feet. If a relationship isn't working, make it work or don't, but don't play the victim by hiding behind your choice to be a consensual slave.

Consensual slavery will take on different permutations as individuals put their own twist on the concept. One owner may enjoy a bratty servant, so long as the brattiness is confined to clearly negotiated situations. Other owners may wish to own slaves who will stay home and care for the house and family. Regardless of the specifics, a consensual slavery relationship remains a relationship between equals that is not egalitarian. While the division of labor may not always be fair, the power exchange is negotiated for the benefit of all parties involved.

Choosing to be a consensual slave is not something to take lightly. This book will help illuminate some of the very real issues consensual slaves face and offer some ideas for how to deal with those issues. This book is not a "how to" or "one and only way" for anyone, but it is a way for those who wish to live a life of consensual slavery to learn about it without diving into the deep end by plunging into a relationship only to find the reality doesn't match their fantasies. This book will provide you with research, discussion and personal anecdotes. It is my hope that you'll be able to take this information, apply it to your own experiences and know that you are not alone in your quest.

Remember that total power exchange relationships, like any other relationship, will have as many varieties as there are individuals engaged in them. What you'll get from this book is honest and frank discussions of the life I live as a consensual slave. Your experiences will vary but I hope the commonalities found in this type of relationship and represented in this book will help you.

If you make the choice to live as a consensual slave, you must accept the responsibility and burden of the multitude of conditions which often accompany that choice. The purpose of this text is, in large part, to help dispel the myths of the consensual slave and to help those who believe the life of servitude is right for them find their way to a successful and happy relationship. I hope that hearing from someone who has already made this choice will help you find your own path.

Conservation of mass. (2007). In Wikipedia [Web]. Retrieved OCT 23, 2007, from http://en.wikipedia.org/wiki/Conservation_of_mass

Why Consensual Slavery?

So why would any intelligent man or woman give themselves mind, body and soul to another person? The answers to that question are as varied as are the members of the contemporary Leather Community[9]. Perhaps you read something that turned you on. Maybe you find yourself looking for opportunities to serve and wish for more consistency in that part of your life. Or maybe you feel called to service for a particular individual. No matter your motivation, know that you are not alone in your choice. You are not wrong or sick for choosing to make yourself available to those you serve. If, after serious thought and soul-searching, you find yourself still drawn to a life as a consensual slave, trust your instincts and grab for the brass ring!

My desire to be a consensual slave arose early in my life. So early I won't tell you how old I was, so as not to shock those who are but newly initiated to the desire. Suffice it to say some of us are drawn toward this life before we even truly understand life as a whole.

I remember my first fantasies. I was kidnapped by evil men who wanted to do me harm. There was always a good guy to save me, but the evil men took me and had their way with me before I was saved. I tied up my dolls, making one evil and the other good. The good girl always got tied up and tortured.

Later, I wanted to be helpless to the whims of my partner during sex. I got lucky enough that my first sexual partner said, "Sure!" when I asked him to tie me up. Later partners were agreeable to varying degrees, but it still wasn't enough for me. When I found the BDSM community, I learned there was more, but the sadomasochistic play lost its appeal in favor of service.[10]

---

[9] Broad term to identify the larger community of BDSM and including both hetero and homo sexual groups and members.

[10] As noted previously, I use the terms Leather and BDSM interchangeably. As such, I consider the community to include more than just play. I see it as having a heavy focus on power exchange relationships as well. Since it is the power exchange that fulfills me, finding the community meant finding power exchange relationships so I could shift from the sexual thrill of play to the life-fulfillment of service.

I serve because I am happiest when I am of use and of value to another. I have learned, sometimes through hard lessons, to be careful how I choose to whom I offer my service. I have also learned that I am completely happy and capable of sustaining that happiness when I am engaged in a total power exchange dynamic with a partner I love and trust.

Consensual slavery can be an outlet for a few hours or a lifestyle for a lifetime. The level and degree to which you offer your life to another depends upon your needs and wants, and the needs and wants of those you wish to serve.

The Relationship with Your Owner: Fantasy and Reality

Fantasy

Do you remember the first time you felt sexual arousal? Do you remember what caused the feeling? I do. I was lying in bed, my panties pulled tight into my crotch and I was pretending I'd been tied up and thrown into the trunk of a car by the bad guy from the latest episode of The Hardy Boys. Sean Cassidy was on his way to save me, but just as he hadn't been able to save the woman he loved in that one episode, he'd be too late to save me too. The bad guys would have their way with me before he found me.

Those types of fantasies have followed me throughout my life. I still fantasize about kidnapping and rape. Do these fantasies make me a freak? It depends on who you ask. I don't feel like a freak and the men I've shared these fantasies with don't think I'm a freak either. Regardless of the specifics of your fantasies, it is important to understand that your preferences in relationships will often come from your fantasies. Are you looking for the knight in shining armor? Do you seek the damsel in distress? Is the school marm awaiting you in her office? Any of these fantasies can be found in consensual power exchange dynamics, but how sustainable are they? At the end of the scene[11], prince charming might have thinning hair and his horse may be a 1979 Volkswagen. Can you sustain your life on fantasy or does your sustenance come from the "meat" of your relationship?

Most, if not all, of us who come to the leather lifestyle do so because it turns us on. We are thrilled by the scent of leather, the caress of the cane, or the sight of a kneeling slave. And while those things are wonderful, they are not sustainable every moment of every day. The rest of your life will intrude on you and your fantasies, leaving you with just the relationship with your partner and without the accouterments of fantasy.

---

[11] A sadomasochistic play term denoting a specified time for participants to engage in a negotiated sharing of activities.

Reality

It is important to treat the basis of any power exchange relationship as you would any other long-term relationship. Do you like the person under the leather? Can you talk to them about your interests and hobbies? Can you listen to them tell you about their dreams? Are you compatible as people? If you can't answer these questions, perhaps you need to take the time to do so before you agree to a power exchange dynamic with this person. As much as we might dream of living every moment of every day chained to the wall in a dark dungeon containing a multitude of delightful torture devices, the reality is we'll have to go to work, walk the dog and spend time in vanilla[12] pursuits with the one to whom we offer our service.

I met the man I am now in service to when he came to the grand opening of the leather club I owned in North Carolina. He came in with a friend and a woman who was in service to him. I remember smiling at him, welcoming them all and then rushing off to take care of something. I also remember thinking he was attractive...he has a nice ass and I'm a sucker for a beautiful smile.

I was involved with another dominant at the time, so I wasn't searching for a relationship. When the man I now serve came to my club regularly over the next few months, we spent time talking and interacting as equals. We grew to like each other and learned that we had a lot of similar thoughts and ideas both in and out of the dungeon. When I was free to seek a relationship, I approached him and we talked and negotiated a lot before we agreed to try a power exchange. The base of knowledge we started with was vast compared to that which I have begun other power exchange relationships with and I think our relationship is stronger and happier because of it.

We still like each other. Some of my favorite times with him are those when we are sitting on the couch just talking. He tells me jokes, I tell him silly stories. We share our hopes and dreams. We enjoy each other's company. I think being comfortable with your partner is one of the most important qualities necessary in order to build a long-lasting power

---

[12] A term used to differentiate between the activities, preferences and lifestyle choices made by mainstream society and those made by members of the Leather Community. Vanilla refers to the choices and mindsets of the mainstream society.

exchange relationship. If you are constantly on edge with each other, you will impede the trust building necessary for power exchange relationships to work. Besides, unless you view these relationships as disposable, why wouldn't you want to spend time with the one you serve whether on your knees or at the grocery store?

I am happily in service to a man who frightens many people. His joking makes me giggle and makes others nervous. His size is comforting to me and intimidating to others. I know him well enough to know when he's not joking anymore or when he's feeling aggressive, so I can adjust my behavior to meet his needs. Had we not spent time with each other outside the power exchange dynamic we now share, I don't think we'd know each other so well. Getting to know people is the only way to ensure you're compatible. So many others have asked me why the man I serve doesn't scare me and my only answer is, I know him and we're right for each other. Taking the time to get to know the person behind your fantasy will help you build a full and longer-lasting relationship, making it far more possible to have the fantasy become reality.

There seems to be such a rush in our community to go from meeting to playing to serving. I've always wondered why this is. Why do we seem to feel as though leathersex[13] relationships should move at a faster pace than vanilla relationships? If you look at successful vanilla relationships, how many of them do you know that began as sex on the first date? I bet not as many as those which resulted from time spent getting to know one another before diving into the heavier aspects of the relationship. Why, then, do so many in the Leather Community think long-lasting power exchange relationships will result from nothing more than a few instant messages and a night of hot leathersex?

I often look at the speed with which relationships in the Leather Community form and dissolve and wonder if our community doesn't view power exchange relationships as disposable. Are we so caught up in the fantasy of leathersex that when the lights come on in the dungeon we realize we've put someone else's face on the person we're with? And if such is the case, what do we do about it?

It is essential to approach relationships within the community as you

---

[13] The wide and nearly inexhaustible variety of sadomasochistic play engaged in by members of the Leather Community. Leather sex may or may not include intercourse.

would those you engage in from your vanilla life. If you are going to engage in a power exchange relationship, wouldn't it be prudent to talk to the prospective partner about long-term goals and dreams? Shouldn't you discuss your desire to remain involved in the relationship in terms that clearly indicate you aren't just waiting for the next best thing?

I will bash you over the head about negotiation many times throughout this book because I truly believe that clear communication prior to engaging in a power exchange relationship can minimize heartbreak later. If you don't know your partner's position on children, what will happen if they tell you they want a baby? If you haven't discussed your desire to continue your education, how will you handle it if your owner says you cannot return to school? And if you envision living in bondage and naked 24/7, what's going to happen when your owner tells you to get a job?

Even as well as the owner and I know each other, sometimes gaps in our discussions arise. For example, a few weeks ago, he made a joke to me about getting pregnant. I kind of freaked out (blame it on hormones since I was about 24 hours from my period) and later realized that what I said made it sound as though I never wanted children with him. I talked to him about it a few days later and he agreed that my words had seemed like a flat no to children with him. We talked and I explained that it wasn't a no so much as a not now. Circumstances in our lives are such that I do not feel prepared to have his child and that he does not feel ready to have another child. When those circumstances change, I know that he wants more children and I am definitely open to having a child with him. Had we not talked, resentment could have built between us over a misunderstanding. Had we discussed children earlier in the relationship, the entire situation could have been avoided. Take the time to talk about life-changing things with your prospective owner so you can hammer out differences before they become problems.

It is important to know the person you offer your service to on an interpersonal level so that when the fantasy fades you aren't left with a stranger. And isn't the fantasy all that much more enticing when you know the person? Isn't it far more thrilling to know when your owner says things that make your toes curl with desire that the person is capable and willing to carry out those things? I know that I revel in the safety of knowing the man I serve will do exactly as he says he will when it comes to his treatment of his property. I don't have to play guessing games with him or wonder if this time he really means it since the last time he said it, he didn't follow through. Because I know the man outside the fantasy, I can trust what he says and does.

I know this book is written with a slave reader in mind, but I want to stress the importance of both sides of the crop getting to know each other as people before and during a power exchange relationship. Owners have fantasies too. Owners put other faces on bottoms when the lights are low in the dungeon, just as servants do. It is crucial to long-term happiness that when the lights come up, both partners see past the fantasy to the true person.

If, as a servant, you find yourself being idealized, it may be helpful to your relationship to talk with your owner about being human. Talk with them about your hopes and dreams and be open to their suggestions on how to reach them. In other words, be yourself rather than striving to be the fantasy. See your owner rather than the fantasy. You'll both be happier in the end.

Fantasies are fabulous. Don't ever let anyone tell you that you shouldn't fantasize and share those fantasies with your partner. Just don't be surprised when vanilla life responsibilities pull you both out of the dungeon and keep you out of it. When that happens, having and continuing to develop a relationship with the person rather than the fantasy will help you be happier and healthier.

Relationship Dynamics

For the purposes of this book, I will discuss three generally recognized dynamics commonly found in the community[14]. The top/bottom dynamic is often a play-based relationship dynamic. The dominant/submissive relationship dynamic is a relationship of minimal power exchange and constant negotiation. The master/slave dynamic is a power exchange relationship built upon negotiation with consent to the relationship rather than the activities of the relationship. Many relationships in the Leather Community build on aspects of each of these dynamics and some relationships even progress through the three dynamics in a process beginning with play and ending with day to day relationship dynamics. This progress is not, however, necessary for any relationship. There is no value judgment in these definitions. One dynamic is not better, fuller, or more real than the others. Rather, they are simply different ways to interact.

Top/Bottom

The dynamic of top[15] and bottom[16] is one often reserved for the playroom or dungeon. Many top/bottom dynamics are such that the participants negotiate a scene, play, and return to their lives without further connection with the other until the next negotiated playtime. While many top/bottom dynamics are part of long-standing play partner relationships, the dynamic itself has little or no element of dominance or submission outside of the negotiated play. Steve Sampson, a leatherman from the southwest, once defined a top as the giver of an action and the bottom as the receiver of an action (Steve Sampson, workshop given at the Master/Slave Conference,

---

[14] I want to quickly acknowledge that there are many other specific dynamics within the Leather Community. You will probably come across, or possibly engage in, dynamics such as Daddy/girl, Mommy/boy, pet/handler, and pony/trainer. These dynamics will often contain many of the same elements of those I've included in this text while maintaining a level of uniqueness that separates them from the dynamics I have discussed. These dynamics have not been included in this text because I do not have experience with them and not because I do not see them as separate from the dynamics I have included.

[15] The giver of an action in sadomasochistic play, often used interchangeably with sadist.

[16] The receiver of the activity during sadomasochistic play, often used interchangeably with masochist

Washington, DC, 2006). If we approach this dynamic from Sampson's standpoint, it becomes much easier to understand the masochistic[17] masters and sadistic[18] slaves we occasionally encounter in the lifestyle. Being a bottom, in and of itself, has nothing to do with dominance or submission. Rather it is an expression of an individual's desire to receive an action from another within the confines of a negotiated leathersex scene. Within the parameters of this definition, the top/bottom dynamic is relegated to exist only in the bedroom, dungeon or playspace.

Dominant/Submissive

Many relationships in the Leather Community may begin as top/bottom relationship dynamics. Once the participants in the relationship spend some time together, they may then progress to a different dynamic, one which includes elements of dominance and submission, although this progression is not a requirement for successful relationships. The dominant[19]/submissive[20] dynamic often transcends the boundaries of the dungeon and may or may not be a part of every day life for the participants in the relationship. In a dominant/submissive dynamic, the submissive member of the relationship agrees to submit to the whims, desires and directives of the other while the dominant member agrees to accept the submission. A dominant/submissive dynamic may involve submission in one or more areas of the submissive's life, but is often not all-encompassing.

Some dominant/submissive dynamics are individually negotiated on a daily basis. As Rick, a member of the submissive/slave panel held at The Cell Block in December 2006, explained, "a dominant/submissive dynamic is one in which the parties are constantly negotiating the level of submission and dominance. Each day, each act, each yes or no, is a new negotiation and the outcome is not predetermined by the participants or prior agreement to said activity." This is not to say that every action or

---

[17] Masochist--A sadomasochistic player who enjoys receiving pain. Often used interchangeably with bottom.
[18] Sadist--A sadomasochistic player who enjoys inflicting pain. Often used interchangeably with top.
[19] In a power exchange relationship, this is the partner who receives power from the submissive.
[20] A gender non-specific term used to identify the submissive member of a power exchange relationship.

request requires negotiation. Rather it means each act and request is open to negotiation. Often couples engaged in dominant/submissive relationship dynamics do not continually negotiate simple matters. Instead, they reserve the right to do so should an issue arise or an action be requested that one or the other is not ready to acquiesce to. It is this element of constant negotiation which differentiates the dominant/submissive dynamic from the master/slave dynamic.

The concept of constant negotiation in a submissive/dominant dynamic should not be confused with bratty behavior or smart ass masochists acting out in order to force their partner to punish them. Instead, think of this ongoing negotiation as situational power exchange. If certain conditions are met (conditions determined by the participants), then the submissive/dominant dynamic is in effect. If the conditions are not met, then the dynamic is not in effect.

For example, a couple agrees to engage in a dominant/submissive dynamic only when they are attending leather events. Should they then decide to attend a local arts festival, they likely wouldn't behave in a manner consistent with the dominant/submissive dynamic you would observe should you see them at a leather event. Situational power exchange can be every bit as intense and consuming as total power exchange. I will caution you, however, that the dominant/submissive relationship dynamic can be tricky to maintain. I say this because it requires the participants to "shift gears" frequently and often on short notice.

When the dynamic is in effect only when certain conditions are met, the necessity of the partners to go from vanilla to leather in short order can, and does, arise. Shifting from the in-charge vice president to the subservient maid can be difficult and may require ritual or time to enact. Many submissive/dominant couples I have known had a ritual or signal they used to help each other move from their vanilla lives to their power exchange relationship. If you engage in such a relationship, I recommend finding the trigger that works best for you.

Master/Slave

The third dynamic is the master/slave dynamic. This dynamic often encompasses elements of the other two dynamics, such as play and a certain level of conditionality, but the main difference is the element of consent. In a master/slave relationship, consent is given for the relationship itself, not individual acts or tasks. As defined earlier, consensual slavery encompasses both free will and consent. When you agree to engage in this type of relationship, you do so with the full knowledge and understanding of a responsible adult engaged in leathersex and BDSM activities. There are no non-consensual slaves in the leather community, despite any claims to the contrary. Responsible adults make choices and must accept the consequences of those choices. If you choose to be a consensual slave, do so, but do not ever think you are less than a responsible adult able to walk away should the relationship not work out.

The negotiation of a master/slave relationship, then, becomes key to the happiness of the participants in the relationship. Without clear negotiation of limits (something we will define and clarify later), expectations, and boundaries, consenting to such a relationship becomes a disappointing, and sometimes dangerous, endeavor. And by dangerous, I'm not just talking about physical harm. Sometimes accidents happen during play and people get hurt. I've had cuts and bruises, marks that have lasted for a week or two. That kind of "danger" most of us can live with. It heals. I'm talking about the emotional danger we put ourselves in when we don't negotiate enough so that our needs are met. Those scars are often deeper and take longer to heal than the physical ones.

Once you've negotiated the expectations of your consensual slavery relationship, you then agree to the relationship rather than individual activities within the relationship. When I agreed to serve the man I now serve, I agreed to be his property to do with as he saw fit, so long as he did not violate my limits. Since my limits have nothing to do with leathersex activities, any such activities he wishes to engage in, I have already agreed to. In turn, he has agreed to the relationship and his obligations to care for and protect me as his property. He does not need to consult me regarding his needs because I have agreed to meet them. He does not need to negotiate a scene in the dungeon because I have already agreed to any activity he wishes to engage in. If this sounds a little scary to you, good! Agreeing to the relationship rather than an activity is an enormous responsibility. I implore you to be certain you have negotiated the relationship you need before you agree to become a consensual slave.

Levels of Power Exchange

It dawned on me as I was writing this chapter that not only are there differences in the dynamics I've discussed already, but there are differences in the level of power exchange in any of those dynamics. As such, I think it is important to also discuss the three levels of power exchange couples might engage in as part of their relationship dynamics. The giving or receiving of power, i.e. submission to the will of another or acceptance of the submission of another, defines the level of power exchange in a given relationship. Relationships might have no power exchange, limited power exchange or total power exchange dynamics.

No Power Exchange

The no power exchange dynamic is often seen in strictly play partner relationships, or relationships where the participants are engaged in leather relationships, not with each other, but with others outside their committed relationship. For example, a top and bottom who play together at sadomasochistic games[21], but do not engage in any type of dominance or submission play would be classified as having a no power exchange relationship. The two slaves engaged in a polyamorous relationship with a single owner might also fall into this category as it applies to their relationship with one another. Neither slave is the recipient or giver of power when it comes to the relationship between them, yet they have a relationship with each other because of the master they serve.

Limited Power Exchange

In a limited power exchange, the participants might negotiate limits based on time or scope. Perhaps the submissive wishes to offer the dominant the right to determine what she eats or wears during a specified time period. Or maybe the negotiation of the relationship included a list of areas over which the dominant has control for the duration of the relationship. The limited power exchange relationship is likely the most common in the contemporary leather community. When the pressures and responsibilities of life are such that total control is not available to either the dominant or

---

[21] Any of the variety of activities engaged in by members of the Leather Community, often involving the giving and receiving of pain.

submissive (i.e. one is married, or lives a significant distance from the other), a limited power exchange relationship can be very fulfilling for both the submissive and the dominant.

Limited power exchange relationships require a significant amount of negotiation in order for them to be successful. Clear definition of the scope and depth of the power exchange will be necessary for boundaries and expectations to be clear. If the limited power exchange is part of a poly relationship, the need for specific negotiation is increased as the boundaries between and among the members of the poly family will have to be defined in addition to the depth and scope of any power exchanges between and among the members.

For example, I once engaged in a limited power exchange relationship with a dominant while I was married to another man. Both men knew of each other as per the negotiations of our polyamorous relationship. Additionally, the dominant and I had to negotiate the depth and scope of our power exchange in such a way that it would not interfere with my responsibilities to my husband. It was a complicated negotiation which had many sessions of renegotiation when problems arose between the dominant and my husband over the power exchange and its affect on me and my responsibilities to both men. Only clear communication helped defuse potential bombs when one partner didn't feel as though their needs were being met.

Taking the time to clearly negotiate all boundaries for a limited power exchange relationship, and being open to renegotiation when problems arise, will help you and your partner be happy in what can be a very complicated relationship. Flying by the seat of your pants and attempting to put out fires rather than negotiating clearly at the onset will likely cause your limited power exchange relationship to fail or, at the very least, be difficult to maintain.

Total Power Exchange

The total power exchange relationship, the focus of this book, is the offering of control of the submissive's entire life to the dominant. It does not mean the submissive is suddenly free from the responsibilities of being an adult, or that the dominant is now responsible for micro-managing the submissive's every waking moment. It does mean that each thought, action, and inaction of the submissive is completed with the knowledge that there are consequences as part of the negotiated consensual slavery relationship in which they are engaged.

As noted above, negotiation of a total power cxchange or master/slave relationship is critical to the happiness of the parties engaged in the relationship. And the participants should not think negotiation is a once and done endeavor. Instead, successful total power exchange relationships operate on the concept that the servant has agreed to give themselves mind, body and soul[22] to the dominant in exchange for boundaries, guidance and clear consequences. When there are human, interpersonal issues between the members of a total power exchange relationship, renegotiation or clarification can return harmony to the relationship.

The total power exchange relationship is not for the faint of heart, but if you prepare for it and work at it (much as you would any other sort of relationship you want to succeed with), it can be intense, sexy, and fulfilling beyond your wildest fantasies.

---

[22] It is important to note that when a servant gives themselves to their owner, they do not stop being the thinking, feeling human being they were before they entered into a total power exchange relationship. Giving yourself over to your owner does not stop you from having thoughts and feelings and opinions. It simply changes how and when you express those thoughts and feelings.

Needs vs. Wants

When you decide you want to begin negotiating a power exchange relationship, one of the first things you will need to do is clearly understand the difference between your needs and your wants or desires. Understanding these differences will help you clearly negotiate your needs and wants and will result in a happier relationship for both you and the dominant.

Needs are those things you must have in order to be healthy in body, mind and soul. Needs are deal-breakers for relationship negotiations. The failure of either member of the relationship to meet the needs of the other can, and likely should, end the relationship. Your needs should include not only the physical needs of the body necessary for survival, but also the emotional needs necessary for your happiness.

Wants are those things you prefer or like. Wants are the icing, the cake, the whole desert to the needs of eating a meal for sustenance. Wants are often the niceties of life and are generally not relationship deal-breakers. However, do understand that if one partner's wants always, and without fail, override the wants and desires of the other partner, the relationship is unlikely to be a happy one. Irregardless of power exchange dynamics, consensual slavery relationships involve real people and often require a level of compromise. If you find that none of your wants and desires are being met in the relationship, talk it over with your owner. Reaffirm that you have shared your wants with your owner and then discuss why they repeatedly go unfulfilled. Perhaps there is a gap in communication and your owner believes he or she is granting your desires. Or maybe your service is not meeting their expectations and so they feel there is no need to reward you. Open communication is necessary throughout a power exchange relationship and should definitely be used when you feel you are being left out of some part of the relationship. Servant or no, our desires are desires for a reason and we deserve to have them granted from time to time.

Some common needs I have presented to dominants with whom I have negotiated relationships include the need for connection, the need to have clear boundaries and structure and the need for the time and place for free speech. I have learned through experience that without these core needs being met, I may continue to serve, but I will be miserable and will eventually self-destruct. Sharing these needs up front, during negotiation, gives a prospective owner the opportunity to either agree to meet my needs or refuse to engage in a power exchange relationship with me.

Some wants and desires I have shared with dominants include the desire to be kept informed should another partner be added to the relationship. I also share my clear preference for men over women as I am a heterosexual woman with no bisexual leanings. Additionally, I share my preference for maintaining my dignity in public and the desire for the dominant to help me with maintaining this stature. Failure on the part of a dominant to meet these preferences and desires is not a deal breaker for me. I may, in fact, ask for time to discuss the issue, but I won't bolt from the relationship over my wants and desires not always being met.

If you are considering entering into a power exchange relationship, I strongly recommend you first write out your list of needs and desires. Be sure you are clear on which is which; make clear your needs so they are met and resolve yourself to the fact that some desires simply won't be met every time. If we are to treat power exchange relationships as we would any other relationship, why would we not begin by making it clear to our partners what we must have in order for the relationship to be successful. Don't set you and your partner up for failure by being unclear about what you need or by being unwilling to compromise on what you want.

This exercise is not only for the submissive partner, but is invaluable for the dominant partner as well. Encourage your prospective owner to complete this exercise too.

Try this:

Complete the following sentences:
Physically, I cannot live without (literally, what can you not survive without?) _____.
Emotionally, I cannot live without_____.

The answers to the first question are likely to be somewhat universal. We all need food, water, and shelter to physically survive this world. However, don't forget other physical needs such as sex and physical contact. While some power exchange relationships are strictly platonic, I know that I would personally be miserable without physical contact with the man I serve. And I am not even referring only to sex, which is fabulous, but rather to physical intimacy. The ability to touch and be touched is important to me. Important enough that it is a need and not a want in my world.

In fact, if you were to review the document I shared with the man I now serve prior to our agreeing to engage in a power exchange relationship, one clause you would find is the specific request that physical contact be continued (as we had been at the "kiss and cuddle" stage prior to this document being written). I explained that past relationships had taught me to be circumspect in my initiation of touch, but that I definitely craved it. I am lucky enough to belong to a man who took me at my word and reaches for me when we are together because he knows I will wait for his indication that touch is appropriate. He is especially good at reading my mood and knowing when I need more touch, such as I did prior to writing this section of the book. My willingness to be open about not only the need for touch but the specifics of how touch has played a role in previous relationships has given the owner enough information to make clear his preferences while meeting my needs.

It is the answers to the second question, the emotional needs you have, which are often the cause of every relationship success and failure, regardless of the type of relationship we are engaged in. There are power exchange relationships in which the participants are not emotionally engaged with each other. There are power exchange relationships where the participants are both lovers as well as owner and servant. Many power exchange relationships fall somewhere in the middle. You must decide for yourself where you are comfortable on that continuum.

Emotional needs, while difficult to express, are central to the health and success of a relationship. It can be especially hard for service-oriented individuals[23] to speak up about emotional needs if they feel as though such needs should be secondary to the needs of those they serve. Regardless, clear expression of and negotiation for the meeting of emotional needs is crucial to creating a successful power exchange relationship. If you fail to communicate your emotional needs, you have no one but yourself to

---

[23] I consider myself to be a service-oriented woman. I find pleasure in serving the needs of those I serve and service is central to my life. There are, obviously, other types of servants who fill other types of needs for their owners.

blame when they are not met.

And even when you think you've been clear about expressing your needs to your partners or potential partners, you have to be willing to revisit the issue should problems arise. Perception is reality but sometimes your perception doesn't match your partner's.

As part of negotiation for a past power exchange relationship, I told my prospective partner I needed to serve a man who was willing and able to make me a part of his whole life. I didn't want to be a secret or a toy; something only brought out when it was convenient or safe to do so.

In my mind, I was clear about needing to maintain an emotional connection with those I serve because a previous relationship had been with a man who hid me from his wife (and the wife from me). I had shared that information with the new prospective owner and believed by indicating a need to be out in the open was the same as indicating my need for emotional connection with my owner. I was wrong. Experience has taught me to be far more specific. Seven months into the relationship with the new owner, I was absolutely a part of every aspect of his life. Everyone knew about me and I held a place in the forefront of his everyday interactions with others.

And I was miserable. He slept on my couch. He had intimate relationships with other women. He rarely touched me, nor spoke to me unless it was to direct me in a task.

I had what I told him I wanted. What I didn't have was what I needed. My inability to clearly say, "I need emotional connection to those I serve in order to be happy and healthy," placed me in an unhappy position. When the situation boiled over into other people's lives and the other relationships he was engaged in, I sought help from someone I respect and trust, Viola Johnson.

Miss Vi asked me if I wanted a lover or an owner and I was forced to admit I wanted and needed both. I absolutely need physical and emotional connection with those I serve or I become resentful of every service I perform. And because of what I learned in that relationship, I now clearly include emotional needs in my negotiations of power exchange relationships. As for that relationship, we ended the power exchange a few months later. Neither of us was wrong or the "bad guy" in the relationship. Rather we both learned an important lesson about clear communication of needs during negotiation of power exchange relationships.

Your needs assessment will require a lot of time and evaluation before you can honestly and completely answer the questions I've presented. And, believe it or not, the answers to these questions will change over time. Perhaps you begin a relationship in which you are a servant but not a lover. Over time, you may discover you need emotional connection. Don't take these changes out on your partner. Rather, renegotiate and communicate. It's always possible that those you serve are having the same change of heart. However, you must also be ready to accept that your partner doesn't want to change their position on an issue. It is at that time you must consider your options and make choices based on your own emotional and physical health.

This book is about consensual slavery. That means that at any time, either partner has the right and obligation to withdraw their consent to the relationship should their needs go unmet. As consensual slaves, we sometimes forget that those we serve are just as, if not more, vulnerable to the vagaries of human emotion as we are. If we stepped into a relationship with someone who did not share his or her needs and wants with us, how can we be sure we can meet them? Push for a clear understanding of your partner's needs and wants during negotiation so you know if you are willing and able to meet them. Much of this book focuses on what a slave should do prior to entering a consensual slavery relationship, but the unspoken caveat to everything I say here is that there is another human being engaged in this relationship with you. Don't focus so much on your own needs and wants that you fail to recognize those of your partner.

Limits versus Social Restrictions

If you've been in the scene for more than five minutes (and I mean that literally), you've probably heard the question, "So, what are your limits?". Do you know how to answer this question? Have you considered, then, how to address "pushing" limits? This chapter will define and address limits and social restrictions, and I must thank Jarrett of North Carolina for helping me to understand the difference between the two terms and the importance of expressing the difference to those with whom we interact in the community.

Limits

A limit is something inviolate. It can be a restriction based on health, emotion, or other criteria. The key here is that limits are not meant the be broken or pushed. Dictionary.com defines a limit as "the final, utmost, or furthest boundary or point as to extent, amount, continuance, procedure." Limits in the Leather Community are those things which will cause irreparable harm to the person. That harm can be either physical or emotional In my case, my limits are: don't mess with my family and don't mess with my job.

My family doesn't know of my involvement in the lifestyle, so to incorporate overt manifestations of my power exchange relationship into a visit to my parents' home would be damaging and would break that limit. Even limiting my availability to my family would have a similar effect as my mother expects to hear from me regularly and see me every few months. The same can be said of my job. I enjoy my career and require the job to maintain my standard of living. Unless a dominant is willing and able to support me, engaging in activities which would endanger my job is simply out.

Limits are not the things you fear because they are unknown. They are the very real, and very known, damaging acts which might arise in a power exchange relationship. A key to defining your limits is knowing to whom you are offering your submission. I know that the man I serve has the medical knowledge to fix any physical damage which I might suffer during a scene. I also know that he is willing to stay with me to fix any emotional damage. Knowing this about the owner makes several limits from previous relationships less valid. And you'll want to remember that a significant portion of your relationship will happen outside the playroom. What limits do you have that have nothing to do with scenes?

Often newcomers to the community will answer the "What are your limits" question with something like, "no animals, children or dead people." Jarrett defined this kind of limit as filler limits.

A filler limit is something spouted off by someone who feels the need to say something other than, "I don't know." If you don't know what your limits are, say so. If you're very new to the scene, people will expect you to have some question as to what your limits are. There is no shame in telling a prospective partner that you are new to the Leather Community and haven't had enough experience to yet know what your limits are. It often takes time to determine your limits, so don't be ashamed if you just don't know. Take some time to develop an idea of what your limits are rather than using filler limits. Filler limits do little to further your education and assessment of what your true limits are. Have you ever seen a pet or corpse rolled out for play during a party? And if you believe the person you are talking to might be a pedophile, why would you want to engage any leathersex activities with them?

Rather than handing out filler limits, take some time to consider what your true limits are. What actions, expectations, or behaviors would cause you irreparable damage. And remember to consider emotional as well as physical damage when you examine limits. Most dominants don't want permanently broken toys, so don't set them up by failing to share limits because you're afraid to sound weak or whiny.

I recommend doing a little research if you are new to the leather scene. Talk to people. Ask them, if it is appropriate to do so, what their limits are, or better yet, how they define their limits. Research online and find out what others consider to be limits and then evaluate their answers and apply that evaluation to yourself.

If someone tells you, as I have, that their only limits are keeping their family and their job out of the power exchange relationship, how does that make you feel? Are you comfortable with that idea for yourself (not for the person who has said this)? Are there other areas of your life you need to keep inviolate?

Remember, if you ask others about their limits, keep your assessment of those limits to how they might fit into your life, not what you think of the limit in general. You may feel I'm crazy to only limit things which might alert my family or my job to my power exchange relationship. And if such is the case, you are certainly welcome to your opinion. However, since limits are personal restrictions, it would be inappropriate to share that type of opinion in any manner other than one which is designed to help you better define your own limits. My limits are my limits and have no affect on anyone but me and the owner. Respect the limits of others, especially if you are learning about them in order to find your own.

I recommended spending time evaluating your needs and wants in a previous chapter. That evaluation will come in handy now as well. What are you unwilling to do in order to have your needs met? That is likely a limit.

Social Restrictions

In contrast to a limit, a social restriction is something you might not prefer, but doing it will not cause you irreparable damage. For example, I might not prefer to have broken bones, but should the man I serve decide to break one of my bones, I wouldn't be irreparably harmed. In fact, the man I serve both can and would repair the physical damage and stick around to work on any emotional damage caused by such an action.

Social restrictions offer the dominant the opportunity to push the boundaries of the servant's comfort zone. Perhaps you have a social restriction on watersports[24]. That gives your owner a place to play, to exert his or her dominance, by engaging in watersports with you. When a submissive in the scene tells a dominant he or she wants their limits pushed, it is really social restrictions to which they are referring. Doesn't it make much more sense to push, break, or violate something that is a preference rather than look for loopholes in definitive negatives? And doesn't it make much more sense to give your owner places where it is

---

[24] A particular sadomasochistic play involving urine.

safe to play rather than asking them to guess which of your limits might be "pushable" and which are absolutes?

Differentiating between limits and social restrictions is the responsible way to approach sadomasochistic play within the boundaries of a power exchange relationship. Be certain you are clear when you communicate these ideas with your owner. If they don't define the terms limit and social restriction the same as you do, be sure to spend some time working with those definitions so you are both approaching the issue from the same position. Failure to do this will likely result in misunderstandings about the pushing of limits.

It is in the area of pushing social restrictions that the difference between a submissive/dominant and master/slave relationship becomes extremely clear. If you have negotiated acceptance to the consensual slavery relationship, the owner need not negotiate individual activities from your social restriction list. You've agreed to the relationship, and so you've agreed to the activities in the relationship that don't violate your negotiated limits even if you find them uncomfortable or distasteful.

Because the man I serve enjoys my discomfort when a social restriction is pushed to the breaking point, activities I would normally say "no" to are those he enjoys testing with me. These activities are not even necessarily those he would normally enjoy or would ever repeat. Rather these are times when I can, and do, demonstrate my ruthless obedience to the relationship. When I comply without hesitation to activities he knows I would rather avoid, I serve his need to receive my obedience and I receive an outlet for my need to obey. Neither of us may actually enjoy the activity, but we are both fed by it.

For example, the man I serve knows I am not bisexual. I have absolutely no interest in women as sexual partners. There have been times, however, when the man I serve has wanted to see if I would obey when it came to sexual interaction with a woman. Despite being both uncomfortable and uninterested in the activity, I immediately complied with his directives. He was fed by my obedience and I was fed by the opportunity to serve. What we got from the activity had very little to do with the activity itself.

As you spend time in the community and attend events, you'll likely come across activities you'll want to add or subtract from your social restriction list. Be sure to share these changes with your partner as doing so will give them the opportunity to either indulge your wants or push your boundaries and indulge theirs.

I recommend using one of the many BDSM checklists available online to get a first line idea of what some of your social restrictions might be. It's also a great tool to share with your partner so they know what you do like as well as what you don't. From time to time, review your checklist. You'll find that what you like and what you think you'd never do will change. There was a time, when I first completed a checklist, that the majority of the items on the list were not just a "no" but a "hell no." Now, there are very few things on the "I'd really rather not, thank you Sir" list and far more things on the "Can we do that again Sir" list.

I'll address self-evaluation in a later chapter, but the concept of evaluation and reevaluation is important to building and maintaining successful power exchange relationships. As your relationship matures, you'll engage in more and more experiences. If you don't reevaluate your ideas and preferences from time to time you may find yourself growing bored and falling into a rut. Chances are, if you're bored, so is your owner. Take the time to go back to your checklists, make adjustments and share that information with your owner. If nothing else, you might just get a hot scene out of the deal as your owner finds some new exquisite torture for you.

Another reason to review your social restriction list is to help find and disarm possible landmines[25]. The more you know about your reaction to certain activities, the better able to cope you'll be. Go to events and parties; watch others play; gauge your response to what others do. These three tasks will help immensely when the one you serve indicates they wish to engage in an activity you have previously indicated is a social restriction. If you already know you're deathly afraid of needles and passed out when you watched a needle-play scene, you can address this with your owner. The discussion may or may not change their mind regarding the activity, but it will give them the opportunity to be prepared

---

[25] Landmines are those explosive emotions triggered by what we do as servants and sadomasochistic players. Landmines can sneak up you and they can sometimes change. I enjoy breath play but after an extended separation from the owner, I was surprised by an emotional landmine reaction to breath play. I cried and struggled and tried to escape the activity I had previously enjoyed on many occasions.

for a strong emotional response from you.

Watching others play with your owner can be beneficial to you as well. It can help you both express your wants and desires about activities, and give you an idea of the likelihood of a particular activity being added to your personal repertoire. I recently watched hook suspension play with the man I serve. His reaction to the suspensions was such that I'm pretty sure I don't have to worry about him engaging in the activity as the bottom. However, the door was certainly left open should he decide to have such suspensions done on me.

The more willing you are to talk to your owner about your feelings and reactions to certain activities, the better able the two of you will be to handle any landmines should they erupt during play. Don't be afraid to share your thoughts on activities with your owner, even if doing so gives them ideas of how to torture you the next time you visit the dungeon. Your negotiations at the beginning of a power exchange relationship should be such that you can trust your owner to care for your mind, body and soul. Sharing your thoughts and feelings gives your owner the information necessary for them to make informed decisions about activities which might interest them.

For example, I was quite frank with the man I serve about my needle phobia. I hate them with a passion, having had bad medical experiences with needles in the past. Because he knows this about me, he knows that should he engage in needle play with me, I am likely to need far more aftercare than I normally do. He also knows, from experience, that I will not tell him no. He's used other medical pointy things on me and has received ruthless obedience from me when he told me to be still. That obedience has been, up to now, enough for him to be satisfied and so he has not engaged in needle play with me. That doesn't mean he won't. It does mean he remains informed about possible landmines and can prepare for them should he decide to poke me with needles.

This chapter is not meant to scare anyone with thoughts of spending time engaged in those activities you most dread. Rather it is to help you figure out what those activities might be and what you will do to cope when you find yourself engaged in them. Not all owners find pleasure in pushing social restrictions, but if yours does, preparation will help you find your way through the activities to the place where your service to the owner is more important than your enjoyment of everything you do with them.

limit. (n.d.). *Dictionary.com Unabridged (v 1.1)*. Retrieved November 02, 2007, from Dictionary.com website: http://dictionary.reference.com/browse/limit

Polyamory

Broad-based families with many members who serve many different roles seem to be on the rise in the contemporary leather community. I don't know if this is a recent change in the community or if I'm just more aware of it now than I have been in the past. I would hazard a guess it is the latter. It has always been my personal philosophy that to expect a single person to meet every one of your needs is not only selfish but also unrealistic. You don't go to a dentist for an ingrown toenail, why would you think a single relationship is going to meet every single need you have in your life? Service based power exchange relationships seem to lend themselves to a polyamorous structure. If one servant is an excellent accountant, an owner probably won't want to occupy his or her time exclusively with household chores. That would likely frustrate both the servant and the served and be a complete waste of the skills which likely attracted the owner to the servant in the first place.

I strongly recommend the book, *The Ethical Slut*[26] to anyone who is engaged in or thinks they might become engaged in a polyamorous relationship. I especially recommend the chapter on jealousy. Because the authors of *The Ethical Slut* did such a fabulous job of explaining poly relationships and describing strategies for having successful poly relationships, I don't want to rehash their book. I will, however, make a few suggestions for poly families in the leather community.

First, be absolutely honest with yourself and your partner before you ever begin talking about opening your relationship. In fact, you should consider the possibility of a poly relationship as you negotiate your relationship from day one. Do not tell a prospective partner you're willing to engage in a poly relationship if you know you are going to be unhappy sharing the one you love or serve.

My first experience with a polyamorous relationship coincided with my first BDSM relationship. I was married at the time and he and I engaged

---

[26] The Ethical Slut: A Guide to Infinite Sexual Possibilities (Paperback) by Dossie Easton (Author), Catherine A. Liszt (Author)
Available from Greenery Press: http://www.greenerypress.com/

in a relationship with another couple. My ex-husband told me and the other couple that he was willing and able to engage in a relationship where the four of us loved each other and had separate and inclusive relationships. The kindest way I can say this is, he lied. Not more than three months into the relationship, he was picking fights because he felt I focused too much on the other couple and not enough on him. The truth was I spent one night a week, if that, with the couple, and the other six days a week with my husband. That was in addition to times when the four of us spent time together.

Ultimately, the relationship with the couple came to an end because my ex-husband admitted he couldn't engage in a poly relationship with them. His inability to admit that a poly relationship was not really something he could live with led to many tears and recriminations and eventually to the ending of a friendship with the couple who introduced me to the Leather Community. Had he been honest when the issue was initially raised, many hours of heartache could have been avoided.

Clearly negotiate the status and interactivity of each member of the household. Be sure you know where you stand and how your standing affects the rest of the household. Are you comfortable engaging in a sexual relationship with your master's other girls or boys? Are you happy being just the domestic help while other family members are engaged in different and separate types of service in the family? I cannot stress enough the need for honesty in these negotiations and clarifications. You'll only make yourself and your family unhappy if you "go along to get along" rather than speaking up for yourself.

The last polyamorous relationship I engaged in prior to the one I currently enjoy was one in which the relationships between and among the members were not clear. The man I was in service to had a regular play partner when we met. I was clear with him that I didn't need him to choose between us, since she fulfilled a need he had that I wasn't too keen on (have I mentioned I'm a massawussy[27]?). Later, the three of us discussed some aspects of the poly relationship, but too many things were left

---

[27] The term massawussy was coined, I believe, during Southeast Leather Fest 2006 by an acquaintance of mine and was originally a reference to the man we both served at the time. It refers to someone who is not a masochist and usually avoids any activity which would result in them being the recipient of pain. I've applied the term to myself since then.

unclear. The play partner and I didn't get along on an interpersonal level for many reasons. The affect that partner had on the owner was detrimental to my peace of mind and therefore to my relationship with him. Later, another relationship was brought in and the confusion grew. Without a clear definition of the role and expectation of each member of a poly relationship with power exchange dynamics, the relationship is doomed to failure.

As a servant, you're likely to want clear boundaries and expectations regarding your interaction with others in the family. It is your right to ask for that in your negotiations. Without those boundaries and expectations, how can you know if you are to serve the dominant your owner is dating? Or maybe you're supposed to act as an alpha slave[28] in the home and delegate tasks to other servants. Negotiation and continued communication will help you remain balanced and happy in your power exchange relationship, even when others are part of the mix.

Address how jealousy will be dealt with. We're human beings, regardless of the role we play in the leather community. Humans are greedy, jealous creatures. Analyze and recognize jealousy triggers and create an acceptable manner of dealing with them. I know any jealousy I feel is triggered by a fear of loss. Simple reassurance on the part of my partner that I am not losing what I treasure is enough to waylay the jealousy and help me find my comfort zone again. Part of the negotiation for a relationship with me includes my ability to say, "I feel..." and have my partner listen to and acknowledge what I say. Those brief moments can often head off major issues if they are addressed rather than ignored. Bear in mind that telling my partner what I feel doesn't mean there will be any change in his behavior. However, I find that if my feelings are acknowledged, I can much more easily adjust to the situation.

I always tell my partners that my imagination is 100 times worse than any reality. Being able to express my feelings about jealousy and fear (while maintaining my station in the relationship) allows the demons to be

---

[28] In many multi-servant households, there is a hierarchy of servants. The alpha slave would be the highest ranking servant in the household. They often have more responsibilities than the other servants because they are in charge of the household as a whole and must delegate tasks and responsibilities to others. The term alpha slave is also used to refer to the servant who is in charge of planning and executing a formal protocol dinner.

brought to the surface and vanquished by the truth. I can't tell you how many times I have built up a jealousy issue in my mind to epic proportions only to present it to my partner and have him laugh and slay the dragon with only a few words. Unresolved jealousy can lead to resentment and anger, misplaced though it may be. It is far simpler to negotiate into the relationship the freedom to express jealousy in a healthy manner than to confront the issue when it is an immediate concern.

If the relationships are clearly defined, as I've suggested above, the dynamic of each relationship can thrive without as many issues arising from other members of the family. Let me explain. If there is one Master and two or more servants, each servant has his or her own relationship with the master. So long as each servant understands both their own relationship and the relationship the others have with the master, they can each be happy in their own relationship. There would be no need to keep a score sheet of what each servant does versus what each servant gets.

For example, if an owner has a servant whose tasks include daily domestic chores and another whose tasks include daily valet services and yet one more who takes care of the household bookkeeping, then the bookkeeper doesn't have to worry about what the maid is doing while the valet is drawing the owner's bath. By the same token, if the master has a sexual relationship with only one of those servants, and that relationship is clearly understood by the other two, there should be no jealousy on the part of the two who do not have the sexual relationship because that is not an expectation of those relationships.

Problems arise when an owner with more than one servant tells the servants they are equal but treats them in entirely different ways. While it is not appropriate for a servant to question the dynamic of the master with another servant, it can be confusing and emotionally devastating to servants when the boundaries and expectations are unclear or clearly unequal. It can be exhausting to be the "good girl" who is punished for the smallest transgression while the "bad girl" gets rewarded for meeting only the most minimal standard. There is no clear solution for this type of situation except to say, negotiate first and hold your partner to your agreements. Push for clear definitions and ask for the level of equity you need in order to be happy.

Poly relationships can be intensely fulfilling or emotionally devastating. The key to success in polyamorous relationships is open communication between and among the members of the family. Be certain that as part of your negotiation for the relationship, you are including the time, place and opportunity to clearly express your feelings about any issues in the relationship. As a servant, you may feel you have no right to speak up regarding the poly aspect of the relationship , however, this is not and should not be the case. Servants are human first and as such must be able to look out for their own best interests when it comes to matters of emotional health. If you find you are unhappy in a poly relationship, it is your responsibility to speak with your owner about your concerns. Enter into that conversation with the full realization that your owner may not be willing to change, but that he or she may be willing to take your feelings into account. If you find your needs still unmet after such a discussion, you need to consider the relationship as a whole.

I'm certainly not recommending that you bolt the first time you and the other servant have a spat. However, if you are truly unhappy, you'll have to reevaluate the entire relationship if your owner indicates he or she sees no reason to change what is causing you harm. As an adult engaged in a relationship you have a certain level of responsibility for the happiness and comfort of your owner, but you also have a responsibility to yourself. Don't let your desire to serve override you need to be emotionally and physically healthy. If you're not happy, speak up!

Negotiation

In any relationship, negotiation is key to the happiness of the participants. We do not luck into finding that perfect person who already knows what we want every time we are in contact with them. Instead, we have to clearly define for others what our needs, wants and expectations are. And we have to be willing to compromise in order to meet the needs, wants and expectations of our partners.

Negotiation for any sort of activity, be it BDSM or business related, must be conducted with the participants acknowledging each other as equals. Just because you identify as a submissive or slave or bottom does not mean you should be any less ruthless in your negotiation than the top, master, or dominant. Prior to the successful conclusion of negotiation, you are not *his* submissive, or *her* bottom. You are two consenting adults wishing to engage in mutually beneficial and pleasurable adult activities. Failure to maintain equality in negotiation can result in resentment and morning after regrets.

Be clear with your partner about deal-breakers. What activities are you morally or emotionally or physically unable to engage in? Don't hedge here. Be clear and stand your ground. If you know you cannot emotionally handle a scene with heavy humiliation, don't say yes to a top who wants to humiliate you just because you really want to play with that person for whatever reason. And remember that either partner in a negotiation can say "no." Just because you're super cute and pretty and everyone wants to play with you doesn't mean the top who wants to humiliate you can't say no to flogging you instead.

Don't enter into negotiation with a set outcome in mind unless you are willing to compromise to get what you want. If a top says to the bottom, "I want to have sex when we finish playing," but the bottom didn't consider sex an option, that bottom then has to reconsider his or her position on the issue or decide if they still wish to play with that top. By the same token, the top who says they want sex following a scene has to be willing to either compromise on the issue or not play with the bottom if the bottom says no.

I cannot stress enough in this discussion the importance of behaving as responsible adults. If you want something, ask for it. If you don't want something, say no...and mean it. You're not engaged in a scene or relationship until the negotiation is complete, so no means no. And don't let your ego interfere with your negotiation. Just because someone doesn't want to do what you want them to do, doesn't make them a bad person and it doesn't make you undesirable. It makes the two of you currently incompatible. And incompatibility is not always a permanent condition.

You'll have to bear with me as I harp on the importance of precision and clarity of language during negotiation. I know that as a slave, I have learned to temper my language and word choice to ensure I am maintaining my station when communicating with those I serve (see the communication chapter for more details on this process). However, negotiations take place before such conventions of communication become necessary. As such, don't defer or be demure in your negotiations. Say what you mean and mean what you say.

Remember that ultimately, you are negotiating your future happiness, be it for the next 20 minutes or the next 20 years. Failure to clearly communicate will lead to a failure of your negotiations and eventually to a failure of your relationship.

As you negotiate, ask for what you want and encourage your partner to do the same. If you don't speak up, how will your partner know what you want to get out of the negotiation? Negotiations are designed to be a give and take of information and the proposal of the exchange of activities for the mutual pleasure of the participants. Without the free-flowing exchange of information, no negotiation can be a success.

And remember that asking for what you want is not the same as demanding it. "I would like the right to meet and get to know any possible additions to the family before they are brought in," is entirely different from, "if I don't like someone you want to add to our family, they don't join us."

If agreed to, both statements have the same probable outcome, but the second is likely to put your partner on the defensive and end negotiations. Both statements clearly indicate your desire to have a level of control over the poly aspect of the relationship, but one asks to be included in the decisions while the other demands total control. Consider which would be your preference if you were on the receiving end of these statements.

I am sure you will approach your negotiations with success as your ultimate goal. However, you do have to face the possibility that your negotiations may not be successful. Your preparations for the negotiations will be key to knowing when it is time to walk away from the table. If you've clearly defined your needs, wants and deal-breakers, you're less likely to get caught up in the moment and agree to something you may later regret. Negotiations can sometimes be like a high-energy auction. Unless you've determined the highest price you're willing to pay before you begin bidding, you run the risk of paying far more than you can afford once you're caught up in the moment.

Should negotiation reach a point of impasse where neither partner is willing or able to compromise, you'll need to consider walking away from the negotiations. Don't compromise on something you'll regret later in favor of instant gratification. If you're prepared to negotiate, you'll be prepared to call it off when it becomes clear that you cannot agree.

Sometimes walking away for a short time is helpful to get negotiation moving forward once again. Perhaps you and your partner have found you cannot compromise on a few issues. Take those issues away from the table and stop negotiation for a few days. During those days away from negotiation, think about the issues and consider possible solutions. When you return to negotiation with your partner, present your solutions and work toward compromise. Don't be discouraged if your negotiations take longer than you might expect. The result of your negotiation is your happiness, make sure you're willing to take the time necessary to make the negotiations successful.

Negotiation is an ongoing part of most relationships. Especially in power exchange dynamics, it is unrealistic to expect negotiation to be a once and done endeavor. Rather, be aware of changes in your needs and be sure to address them with your partner. Power exchange relationships are not disposable. They require work and diligence. If you're willing to go that extra mile, you'll find yourself in much happier and healthier relationships.

A Practical Exercise

Negotiation is an art and skill which will require time and practice. This exercise is similar to the one in the Needs vs. Wants section of the book, but will help you convert your needs to statements for use during negotiation.

- Go back to your list of needs from the earlier exercise.
- From your list, choose a need.
- Using that need, write two statements.
  - The first statement should be a straightforward statement of your need. Make this statement read as though you would not negotiate the point. This is your demand
  - The second statement should be filtered so as not to be confrontational. Rework the first statement to be phrased in such a way that you are still indicating your need but doing so while leaving room for negotiation.

The purpose of the two statements is to understand the difference between voicing your needs and stating an un-negotiable point. While having your needs met in your relationship is important, being willing to negotiate on the specifics of how your needs are met and being able to communicate that willingness during negotiations is just as important.

Playing Without a Safeword

When you negotiate a relationship rather than a scene, as many consensual slaves do, you may find yourself playing without the safety net of a safeword[29]. For those of us who came to the Leather Community relatively recently (such as myself, having been active only seven years), the safeword sometimes takes on epic and heroic proportions. It is the single word that can transport us out of something we are not enjoying without recriminations on the part of the top. But in consensual slavery power exchange relationships, the safeword is often no longer an option.

For example, the "safeword" in my current relationship is some

---

[29] A safeword is an arbitrary word used by players during sadomasochistic activities. Safewords can indicate both a need to stop and a willingness to continue any activity.

unpronounceable medical term that even if I could pronounce it, I'd be unlikely to remember what it was in the midst of a scene. It's a joke among the members of my leather family and nothing more. I know that when the man I serve wishes to play, he will do so for as long as he wishes and I will be along for the ride so to speak. I also know that should I reach the point of being unable to continue, I can speak up and he will consider my wishes. That is what our relationship negotiations have included.

Often partners who have been together for some time find they do not need safewords. They know each other well enough to read both body and verbal cues and stop activities without a safeword. Additionally, some players simply do not wish to have the "safety net" held under them that they feel safewords provide.

There are a few myths about safewords I wish to dispel here. The first is that without a safeword, a top might seriously damage or kill a bottom. This myth is ridiculous for several reasons. First, if you're afraid a top will kill you, you probably ought not play with him or her. Second, a safeword is not a suit of armor. Having one doesn't guarantee your safety in a scene. Only your negotiations and the skills of your partner can do that. Even then, there are accidents and people get hurt. Third, if you have a safeword, but don't use it, you can be just as harmed as if you didn't have one (or did have one and did use it). The point is, the word means nothing. It is what the word has come to represent that matters. Solid negotiation and trust in your partner far outweigh the power of a safeword.

The second myth is that safewords are only for bottoms. The truth is, whether or not you've negotiated the use of a safeword for a scene, either the top or the bottom has the right, as a consenting adult, to stop the scene at any time. Yes, tops get to stop scenes too.

The third myth is that only crazy people play without safewords. To be honest, from the outside a relationship of total power exchange and consensual slavery may appear crazy, with or without safewords. However, consider what it is that we do from a vanilla society viewpoint. I bet we all look a little crazy from there.

Safewords are a tool. They are used by players to set clear boundaries and stops during what can often be very intense play. To use a safeword or not is the choice of the consenting adults engaged in the scene. If you have clearly negotiated the scene, been upfront and honest with your partner about your health and limits, and are willing to use language carefully, safewords are not imperative for the safety of the participants. If, however, you feel more comfortable having a safeword in a scene, make sure you are clear about that preference in your negotiations.

I sometimes wonder what is wrong with using precise language, even during a scene. I came to the community nearly seven years ago and have always advocated the "say what you mean" axiom . Now I do understand that resistance, kidnapping or coercion scenes would require other standards of language, but why not just say "stop" when you no longer want to continue a scene?

The second man I served in this community was also the first to do more than what I would consider slap and tickle play with me. I remember negotiating with him for our first scene. I told him I used neither "ouch" nor "no" lightly. If I said them, I meant them. He took me at my word and then discovered during our scene that I had been absolutely honest with him. I don't remember saying "no" at all and only said "ouch" when the activity reached pain levels I could no longer handle.

As I recall this story, I am left wondering if the reason our community places such emphasis on safewords is because so few people say what they mean. If tops and bottoms use language to manipulate each other into getting what they want, then the only clear constant is the use of stoplight colors[30] to indicate their willingness or unwillingness to continue to engage in the negotiated activities.

I advocate clear and comprehensive negotiation rather than reliance on safewords. However, it is up to you and your partner to make the ultimate decision. And remember, a word is only as powerful as you believe it to be.

---

[30] Many players use the stoplight colors of red, yellow and green for safewords. Red indicates stop, yellow slow down, and green keep going or increase intensity.

Communication

So much can be said by just the way we hold our bodies or the inflection of our voices that communication can be both the cause and solution for a majority of issues which arise in power exchange relationships. Intellectually we know there are appropriate modes, tones and words to be used within the confines of our relationship. The reality is, however, that sometimes our mouths outrun our brains.

How many ways can we say, "Yes, Sir?" There's the one which is merely agreement with what Sir has said. There is the one which indicates our frustration with a task. There is even then one, often accompanied by the raising of an eyebrow, which loosely translates to "You've lost your ever-loving mind, Sir." Two words and a nearly inexhaustible number of translations. No wonder we're often confused by what we hear others say.

As a member of a power exchange relationship, the servant or submissive is often faced with not only the normal human confusion which accompanies the use of the English language, but also the limitations placed on them by those they serve as to appropriate methods, modes, tones and words to be used for communication in the relationship. A previous relationship of mine included the protocol of no use of profanity. Others are asked to speak of themselves in third person. Still others are expected to maintain a certain distance and station at all times except for clearly defined and structured moments when free speech is permitted.

The mantra of our community is "communicate" but so often the problems we face in our relationships stem from either miscommunication or lack of communication. We say things we don't mean, or we say them in ways that are detrimental to our meaning and then wonder what happened. Communication within the boundaries of a consensual slavery relationship has its own issues, including the need for the servant to maintain his or her station while still communicating clearly. Such requirements mean learning new communication skills.

Deference and Diplomacy

Deference is "respectful submission or yielding to the judgment, opinion or will of another" (dictionary.com, n.d.). Knowing when to give in, to put aside your desires in favor of those of your owner, is a skill every servant must learn. Coupled with this skill is the need to learn to let go of things once you've discussed them with your owner. If you defer to him or her, you cannot hold a grudge about that decision.

The use of diplomacy in speaking with our owners helps us find appropriate ways to disagree with them. There is an enormous difference between, "Sir, I think you're wrong," and "Sir, perhaps if we approach the problem this way instead, we'll be more successful." The first is antagonistic and confrontational. The second is a diplomatic way of saying the same thing. The second also offers the owner the right and ability to express his or her opinion without first having to deal with an insolent servant.

Used in conjunction with each other, deference and diplomacy will likely occupy a majority of a servant's day to day communication. An owner who expects a servant to be fluent in the use of deference and diplomacy is not indicating an unwillingness to communicate. Rather, they are being explicit in their expectation that their property remain respectful in communication methods.

Non-verbal Communication

We communicate so much without ever saying a word. The way we stand, the tilt of our head, the set of our shoulders all tell far more than our words ever could. If you've ever wondered how your owner knew something was wrong despite your every effort to verbally convey otherwise, you were likely given away by your body language.

Just as words can be confrontational and inappropriate in a power exchange relationship, so too can body language. I learned this first in the dojo where I studied Taekwondo in college. Prior to working in that school, I often stood with my arms crossed across my chest. I wasn't being purposefully confrontational, rather I was hiding behind my arms. My instructor pointed out to me that in his home school, such a stance was an open invitation for anyone to drop me on my ass.

I have been far more aware of my body language since then, but it was my engagement in power exchange relationships that made me even more aware of the affect my posture and stance might have on others. My tendency during play is to curl in on myself and clench my fists. The man I serve pointed out to me that a fist is a silent defiance and was inappropriate for me to display. I've caught myself closing my hands since then and have immediately opened them.

Your owner may have certain body positions and stances he or she expects you to use or avoid. Be aware of their preferences and abide by them. But also be aware of your own habits and examine them for confrontational elements.

Using inappropriate body language can act as a block to clear communication in a power exchange relationship. If your owner feels confronted by just your body language, he or she is less likely to listen to your words. You also leave them little room for accepting your position if they are unhappy with your presentation.

Explanation versus Excuse

I don't make excuses for mistakes I might make in my power exchange relationship. Excuses are "a plea offered in extenuation of a fault or for release from an obligation" (dictionary.com, n.d). If I have failed to complete a task, or did not meet an expectation I do not expect to be released from the obligation of meeting that expectation. Instead, I will often offer a simple explanation.

Be sure to discuss the use of excuses and explanations with your owner so you are both on the same page. The first time I offered the man I serve a simple explanation for a task I failed to complete, it did not go over so well. I addressed it with him later, apologizing for the tone in which I delivered the explanation (which was a simple, I forgot), and explained that rather than offer an excuse, I was simply telling him what had happened. Once we discussed this, the situation was diffused. If your owner expects more information than you share with them, failure to give it to them is a failure to follow directions.

There is nothing inherently wrong with either excuse or explanation, just be sure that you and your owner have the same expectations about responses to a failure to meet expectations.

The Fine Art of the Apology

Closely related to excuse and explanation is the apology. As a servant, there will come a time when you fail to meet an expectation and after the excuse or explanation, you'll need to apologize. Apologies are an art form in that there are many ways to present them, from simple to highly elaborate.

Martha Beck, in an article for O magazine, offers a four part method of apology which can be easily applied to a power exchange relationship. Beck's (2004) steps are: A full acknowledgement of the offense, an explanation, a genuine expression of remorse, and an offer of reparations for damage.

A full acknowledgement of the offense can be exquisitely painful. It is human nature to wish to minimize our own faults. However, if the servant fully and completely discloses his or her part in the failure which led to the need for an apology, the owner is much more likely to be open to the apology than if they feel the servant is hiding some portion of their responsibility. Always accept responsibility for what you've done, or failed to do.

Offering a simple explanation helps both you and your owner "understand why you misbehaved and assure[s] both of you that the offense won't recur" (Beck, ppg 11, 2004). Understanding yourself and helping your owner understand you will make avoiding the same issue much easier in the future. Give your owner the best information you have and he or she will likely be able to help you better meet expectations next time.

Expressing genuine remorse is important to rebuilding trust. Unless you express true remorse, your owner is likely not going to begin to forgive your transgression. Failure to express or feel remorse is failure to accept responsibility for what you've done.

Offering to make reparations, even if nothing physical has been harmed is an important part of rebuilding trust after it has been broken. Listen to your owner and what he or she might believe are appropriate reparations. Keep an open mind about those reparations and do what you say you will do to repair the broken trust.

Remember that regardless of the method you use to deliver an apology, it is unlikely to get you out of punishment for failing to meet an expectation. The best defense against needing to offer an apology is to work hard to meet your owner's expectations. If you fail to do so, own up to it and accept the punishment offered by your owner. Be willing to accept said punishment with grace and work to avoid similar situations in the future. It is also important to talk to your owner and negotiate into your relationship the letting go of hostilities when apologies have been given and punishments accepted and completed.

I know I am often harder on myself than any owner would be when I feel I have failed to meet their expectations. It is important to me and my mental health to be able to accept punishment and let go, rather than continuing to punish myself. Do not remove the right to finish with a punishment from your owner. Rather accept their punishment as an ending to the situation and move on.

Know, too, that your owner may need closure to the issue. Their administration of the punishment may be their method of letting go of the situation and moving on. Give this to them graciously and then let go with them. You'll both be happier and healthier in the end.

Your owner may have expectations about the time and presentation of an apology. I've seen very ritualized apologies that were beautiful to behold. I've seen simple apologies that were sweet and appropriate. The key to an affective apology is true remorse.

You should never apologize for something if you don't mean it. Better to stand your ground on the issue and face the consequences than to offer a false apology. I'm fairly certain the dominants I've served would far prefer a solid, "No, I'm not sorry" than a false apology.

Suggestions for Clear Communication

Communication issues have been raised throughout this book. My primary recommendation for clear communication is to use clear, precise language and say what you mean. Choose your words carefully so that you are saying exactly what you mean. If you feel limited by your current vocabulary, start reading! We don't learn new vocabulary by osmosis. Instead, we read and look up words we don't recognize. If you choose your words with care, using only those you know and those which meet your needs, you'll have fewer misunderstandings between yourself and those with whom you communicate.

Take time to think before you speak. I know that those we serve expect an answer in a prescribed time frame, but it is advisable to take a moment to think about what you're going to say before you say it.

I know that the first thing to enter my mind when I've been asked a question is likely less than appropriate. Because I know this about myself, I've addressed this issue with those I serve. I have asked for permission to take a moment to compose my thoughts before responding to the owner. I have been granted that permission after carefully explaining that my hesitation to speak was not so I could formulate an answer I think the man I serve wants to hear, but rather so I can phrase the answer I have in an appropriate manner.

Sometimes the first thing to come to mind is, "Sir, you're fucked in the head." I'd rather not face the wrath that answer would get me. I also won't change my viewpoint on the issue, but would instead answer with, "I don't understand your point of view, Sir. Perhaps you could explain it more?"

Choosing the more diplomatic and tactful response in such an instance is likely going to result in a far more positive outcome than the initial response would. Diplomacy and deference, as noted above, really do help mitigate the strong-willed responses servants may need to communicate to their owners.

How Your Owner Communicates

This chapter has dealt with the conventions and practices of communicating with your owner, but it is now time to discuss how your owner may communicate with you. Of course, the communication from your owner will vary, as individuals vary, but I've found a few commonalities in my past relationships.

Learn what your owner means by phrases like "a little while." My first long-term power exchange relationship was with a man who meant anything from two hours to two weeks when he said, "a little while." Later relationships have borne out that this particular phrase is common and generally means an extended time period, longer than an hour.

I mention this particular example because failure to understand what is meant by phrases such as this can lead to a lot of waiting and heartache. I think owners forget, sometimes, that their servants really do wait for them when they are told there will be an answer or further instructions coming. Knowing how long to wait before being annoyed or contacting them can be valuable information for maintaining your sanity.

I also recommend discussing with your owner the destructive power of hope. I far prefer a definitive "no" to a "maybe." While I may be disappointed with the "no," I can get over it and move on because it is a definitive answer. "Maybe" leaves the door open for hope and stretches out the disappointment. I've rarely been in situations where maybe didn't really mean no anyway, so why drag it out and leave me to hope that what I've asked for is possible?

Making it Work

As an English teacher, I am often faced with the woeful state of communication in main-stream society. I see adults who cannot compose coherent simple sentences and who really don't seem to care how difficult it is for the recipient of their thoughts to decipher them through their poor use of the English language. Clear communication is key to any successful relationship, be it father/child, boss/employee or master/slave. I strongly recommend that if you feel you are not a good communicator that you go out and educate yourself. Take a few classes or read until your eyes burn. Look for learning opportunities and take advantage of the resources in our own community. When a communication workshop is offered, go. Take notes and talk to people after the workshop.

One of the best communication workshops I have ever attended was presented by Master Rickford and slave kimmie during their title year[31]. It was a workshop on the differences in the way men and women communicate. That workshop was nearly five years ago and I still

---

[31] Master Rickford and slave kimmie were the Southeast Master/slave couple for 2004. During their title year, titleholders are required to travel and present educational workshops throughout the community. The workshop I am referring to was held at a private function for an eastern North Carolina group.

remember it and use what I learned from it. I implore you to do the same. Don't expect great communication skills to suddenly appear in your brain. Go out and learn, and then apply what you've learned to your relationships. I bet you'll be happier for having done so.

Beck, M (2004, September). Always apologize, always explain. Retrieved November 5, 2007, from CNN Web site: http://www.cnn.com/2007/LIVING/personal/07/11/always.apologize/index.html?imw=Y

deference. (n.d.). Dictionary.com Unabridged (v 1.1). Retrieved November 02, 2007, from Dictionary.com website: http://dictionary.reference.com/browse/deference

Protocol, Etiquette and Ritual

I need to begin this chapter with a note that if you are hoping to find the end-all, be-all of protocols for your own relationships here, you are about to be sorely disappointed. There is no BDSM protocol accepted in every place and for every relationship. There just isn't. Protocol is a very personal thing that cannot be universally applied to our community. Etiquette, on the other hand, is more broadly applicable.

Perhaps I should begin with defining the two terms so we are on equal footing for this chapter. Often we hear in our community that protocol and etiquette are interchangeable terms, however, if that were the case, we wouldn't need both words.

Defining Protocol

Protocol encompasses the rules and standards of a given relationship. These rules and standards may or may not contain elements of etiquette or ritual and are often conditional based on the environment in which the servant finds him or herself. It is protocol which determines things like speech modes, standards of address, and the day to day operations of the servant. Protocol sets up the expectations for behavior in given situations so that should the servant be on his or her own, he or she still knows what behavior is appropriate. Protocol allows the servant the security of the relationship standards inside and outside of the direct control of the dominant.

For example, protocol would tell a servant that he is to address all dominants as sir or ma'am unless otherwise directed by the dominant he is addressing. Regardless of the presence of this servant's owner, the expectation is that he will continue to use the correct mode of address. Being conditionally driven based on appropriate environment, should the servant encounter a dominant in an environment where such modes of address were inappropriate, protocol allows the servant to refrain from using them.

It is the aspect of conditionality that allows protocol to bring the power exchange relationship out of the bedroom to become part of the servant's every day life. Where ritual requires the repetition of tasks in a particular manner regardless of condition or environment, protocol allows for the consideration of condition prior to enactment. Think of a Catholic crossing him or herself. They likely don't consider where they are or under what circumstances they are living before they perform that ritual. Were it a protocol instead, however, conditions and environment would make a difference.

Consider the protocol, "you will remain nude in my presence at all times." A protocol such as this can be lots of fun in the bedroom but it isn't very practical when you're grocery shopping. Additionally, it might be a problem even at Leather Community events as some groups have rules forbidding nudity. Protocol, as defined in this chapter, allows the servant to take into account the environment and other factors before fulfilling the protocol. If the environment is such that it is inappropriate to be nude, the servant may confidently don clothing without fear of reprisal for breaking a rule.

Defining Etiquette

Etiquette, on the other hand, addresses the niceties of interpersonal interaction. Dictionary.com defines etiquette as "conventional requirements as to social behavior; proprieties of conduct as established in any class or community or for any occasion" (n.d.). Here we can see where the idea of a universal BDSM protocol might come from.

Because there are certain social niceties expected in nearly any situation, the etiquette expectations at leather events can appear to be quite standardized. Add to the over-all social niceties the fact that many BDSM and leather organizations have similar expectations of attendees and the myth that there is a single BDSM protocol is born and perpetuated. The truth is, even though such standards of etiquette give the appearance of standardization, each group or organization will have its own specific etiquette and protocol expectations.

Etiquette is defined by the norm of a given group. Therefore, what is accepted etiquette at one leather event may not be accepted at another. If you are unsure of the etiquette at a particular event, ask. If you're uncomfortable with a particular etiquette, you may wish to address it with the group leaders or perhaps not attend their events. Most leather events and groups I have attended strive for etiquette standards which help attendees feel comfortable in what can often be an intimidating environment.

I have found that for the most part, the use of the broader societal niceties will stand you in good stead at any leather event, even if you are unaware of the specifics for the group. To borrow an idea from Robert Fulghum, author of *All I Really Needed to Know I learned in Kindergarten*, the use of any of the following standards will often put you on the right side of any group's etiquette expectations:

*Put things back where you found them
*Clean up your own mess
*Don't take things that aren't yours

I would also add "be polite" to the list. You don't have to kiss anyone's feet or be subservient to anyone you do not belong to, but a modicum of polite behavior will take you a long way in this community.

When Standards Differ

Etiquette standards will often vary from one small community to another, while protocol will vary from one couple to another. Occasionally, this variance can cause the grinding of teeth, but in the end, since protocol is designed to make your relationship work smoothly, if it doesn't meet the standards set forth by another person, that's not your issue, so long as you aren't violating the etiquette of the group you are attending.

For example, at one time I was engaged in a power exchange relationship in which a protocol of no profanity was in place. When that relationship ended, the ties to the protocol ended as well. However, the interaction between me and that dominant did not end. When I would later use profanity in his presence, it always made that dominant cringe. However, since I was no longer held to his protocol, there was little he could do about it. The protocol of my current relationship had no such ban, therefore, my protocol was not being violated.

This is not to say I am suggesting that you purposely flaunt your differences in protocol to make others uncomfortable (though I must admit there were times when I did exactly that...remember, I am human and humans are often petty). Instead, I am hoping you will understand that it is protocol that allows certain servants to behave in one manner while others behave in what would seem to be contrary ways.

Once you and your partner have decided upon the appropriate protocols for your relationship, you will find that having them makes it easier to be secure in your relationship and your chosen station. Knowing the rules always makes finding my place in a new situation easier for me. Going to a leather event can be stressful, especially for servants. Knowing and abiding by your protocols will give you a familiar base from which to work and should help reduce your stress levels.

Developing Protocol

I know this portion of the protocol chapter might seem better suited to a book for dominants, however I believe two things. One, owners choose servants because they believe them to be capable, intelligent people. Two, personal protocols are useful whether a servant is in a relationship or not.

Since protocol addresses behavior, while etiquette addresses the manner in which the behavior is performed, this exercise will look only at behavior, not the niceties of how that behavior is enacted.

First, make a list of behaviors you find comforting, attractive or useful. Be as broad-based and complete as possible in this list. Include behaviors you may have observed, as well as those you may perform already.

For example, my list might include using polite forms of address for people I've just met, offering simple services to all who need them, and remaining quiet in the face of conversation between dominants.

I have always used Sir or Ma'am when addressing people I've just met. I even did that when I worked in retail many years ago. There is a certain comfort to that form of address for me since it allows the other person to offer a less formal alternative rather than relying on any non-verbal clues as to their station or preference.

Offering simple service does two things for me. First, my comfort zone is always in service. If I can get a drink for someone rather than stand or sit alone waiting for someone to request service, I am far more comfortable. Second, it demonstrates, without a doubt, my chosen station within the community.

Staying quiet and unobtrusive is a personal behavior pattern for me that is both comfortable and useful. I learn an awful lot just listening to people talk. If I were to interrupt all the time, I wouldn't learn nearly as much. Additionally, I personally subscribe to the axiom that servants should neither be seen nor heard unless invited to speak. Unobtrusive service is important to me and if it means waiting for a conversation to halt or pause before completing a task, so be it.

The next list you'll want to make is one of behaviors you find stressful, unattractive or counter-productive. This list is important to help you gauge the types of behaviors you wish to avoid.

Personally, I find all bratty and attention-seeking behavior intensely unattractive. It makes my skin crawl and sets up stress reactions like increased heart rate and general agitation.

Remember that just because you put a behavior on your personal lists doesn't mean your partner or future partners will agree with you. Some owners enjoy bratty servants. Others may not want you to remain unobtrusive in your service. Protocol is intensely personal and can only be agreed upon by those engaged in a relationship.

Once you have made your lists, it's time to start sorting them. Group the behaviors on each list together based on their similarities to each other. You'll be developing groups of behaviors to be included in single protocols so your protocol doesn't read like a dos and don'ts list and needn't be three miles long.

I recommend looking at the groups of behaviors and finding a good term to label each group with. Doing so will help immensely with the next step.

Once you've grouped the behaviors and labeled them, it is time to rephrase the labels into directives. Perhaps you have a label of "communication" and that label includes the behaviors of using modes of address, talking with your owner about issues, and refraining from discussing your relationship particulars with outsiders. Your directives may become:

*Address all dominants as Sir or Ma'am unless otherwise instructed.

*Keep your owner informed of all issues, relationship related or not.
*Do not discuss the particulars of this relationship with outsiders.

Notice how the directives are taken directly from the behaviors but say nothing about the method to be used to complete the directive. Doing this allows the enactment of a behavior (making it a protocol) without the imposition of either etiquette or ritual. Working out a protocol without the inclusion of ritual or etiquette allows the personal preferences of the members of the relationship to be enacted while leaving the basic structure in place.

I advocate completing this exercise even if you are not in a relationship because it will help you maintain your chosen station, that of a servant, even when you are not serving a particular owner. Additionally, we have to recognize that many dominants do not complete this exercise for themselves, despite knowing how much more efficient servants are when they have clear boundaries and expectations. Being able to share a personal protocol with a prospective partner demonstrates your seriousness in undertaking the task of becoming a consensual slave and your dedication to the success of such a relationship. Just don't be surprised if the dominant in question makes serious changes to your personal protocols to meet his or her needs.

Levels of Protocol

While protocol defines the overall rules of behavior for a relationship, those rules must have some flexibility depending upon the environment in which the servant finds themselves in. For that reason, many power exchange relationships include levels of protocol. My understanding of these levels comes, in great part, from discussions on the topic with Jarrett of North Carolina.

Informal Protocol

Informal protocol generally address the interpersonal protocols between servant and owner. This is the protocol of day-to-day interaction between the servant and owner. Often, informal protocol is more lax in its strictures than one might believe. It is the language and behavior of a couple with or without power exchange as they go through the daily tasks of their lives. Often, informal protocol is more difficult for a servant than one might think. The more lax the rules, the fewer clear boundaries there are. As I discussed previously, boundaries are important for healthy servants and when boundaries are lax, there can be problems. The key to successful use of informal protocol is consistent application of consequences should expectations fail to be met. Just because the servant is on informal protocol does not mean they should be fully released from their duties.

Public Protocol

Public protocol is what we most often observe between servant and owner when they attend leather events in the community. It is more formal than what might transpire between partners in their home, but still allows for comfortable intercourse between the servant and other attendees. Generally, I have found that public protocol is a comfortable place for me, especially when I am in an unfamiliar environment. The reversion to more formal forms of address and the allowance for my return to unobtrusive service keeps me in my comfort zone.

Formal Protocol

Formal protocol is often reserved for either special occasions or punishment. Formal protocol includes very strict modes of speech and a suspension of the servant's wants and needs in favor of the owner's goals. Formal protocol can be a learning tool for both the servant and the owner as the owner has the opportunity to closely observe the servant without concern for his or her comfort. I've only ever been held to the strictures of formal protocol once. I participated in a protocol dinner held at APEX[32] in May 2006. It was illuminating to me to see how suspension of everything but the needs of the owner (or in this case, all the dominants in attendance) can help servants find the best of themselves. Servants who had previously been uncomfortable working with any dominant other than their own found that they were accomplished regardless of the recipient of their

---

[32] The Arizona Power Exchange (APEX) is a not-for-profit corporation that provides education, social opportunities, and support for adults who are interested in Bondage and Discipline; Dominance and Submission; and Sadomasochism (BDSM) who value individual responsibility, integrity, confidentiality, and respect for self and others. APEX provides on-going forums for education and practice of BDSM and opportunities for like-minded individuals to socialize, explore and learn in a respectful and dignified environment. APEX welcomes all sexual orientations, consensual relationships, and risk-aware BDSM and sexual practices.

service.

The choice to use levels of protocol is, of course, your owner's. I've been involved in power exchange relationships where the levels were clearly defined and used and others where they were apparent, but not specifically defined. As you develop protocol or discuss protocol with your owner, ask about levels of protocol and find out what the expectations are in given situations. Doing so will help you be confident in any environment and enable you to give your best service with confidence.

Ritual

Rituals are designed to help masters and slaves find beauty in what it is that we do. Ritual can be comforting as well, helping us maintain headspace and station.

Watch others, observe their rituals. Do you like them? Can you use them? Would you change them? Do you notice what those rituals do for those who perform them? Answering these questions will help you develop your own rituals to feed you and those you serve.

Find those rituals which help you an your partner find your headspace and use them. I know there is a distinct shift in my own headspace when the man I serve chooses to lock a collar around my neck. There is an accompanying shift when that collar is removed.

I will caution you, however, not to become too dependent upon ritual. I know I am a creature of habit and that deviations from my daily rituals and procedures can leave me grumpy. Because I know this about myself, I try not to depend on ritual to put me in the right head space when I am serving. Instead, I try to maintain that headspace on a day-to-day basis and see ritual as a special set of activities which increase the pleasure I get from serving.

Protocol, etiquette and ritual all play a role in how we interact with our owners and others in the community. The odd thing about these three aspects of power exchange relationships is how they can be intensely different from one relationship to another. So much of your owner will be present in his or her protocols that you'll likely not ever see two protocol lists which are identical. But identical or not, many will have similarities.

Most owners want well-behaved, competent and confident servants. Their protocol, etiquette and ritual expectations will help you become the well-behaved, competent and confident servant of their dreams. Use the tools your owner gives you to your best advantage.

etiquette. (n.d.). Dictionary.com Unabridged (v 1.1). Retrieved November 01, 2007, from Dictionary.com website: http://dictionary.reference.com/browse/etiquette

Fulghum, R All I really needed to know I learned in kindergarten. Retrieved November 1, 2007, from Peace, non-violence, The Canadian Centres for Teaching Peace Web site: http://www.peace.ca/kindergarten.htm

Types of Service

As a consensual slave, you will have to make a decision regarding the types of service you will offer to your owner. This decision encompasses more than the kinds of sexual activities you're interested in, it also requires you to consider the differences between and the appropriateness to the situation of anticipatory, directed and intrusive services. Remember, too, that your owner will share his or her preferences with you. While you may be expecting one type of service to be prevalent in your relationship, your partner may expect another. Be sure to address this issue during your negotiations.

Directed Service

Directed service is service which results from a directive from your owner. Your owner tells you to clean the bathroom and you do so. That is directed service. A large percentage of your day may be taken up with directed services if your owner is one to micro-manage your activities. Do you have a list of daily tasks? Are you expected to complete certain tasks at certain times? These would be considered directed services as well.

There are implied directed services as well. Has your owner indicated a preference for a type of clothing for you to wear? There is an implied directive in that expression of preference. He or she wishes to see you in that clothing. Implied directives can be tricky at times. It is here that clear communication becomes key to your ability to complete even implied directives. The man I serve has clearly told me he does not make suggestions. I have come to understand him to mean that even if something he says has the tone and demeanor of a suggestion, it is an implied directive.

For example, the man I serve has often said he is a "neat freak." The implied directive in that statement is that my home and car must be clean at all times so he is comfortable in those environments. Implied directives can be difficult to follow if you and your owner do not know each other's communication styles. My best advice to you in regards to implied directives it to ask your owner. If you hear something that sounds like an implied directive, ask them, "Do you want me to do X?" Doing so will clarify that particular situation and help you better identify implied

69

directives in the future.

Directed service can run the gamut of fulfilling to exhausting, depending on the type of servant you are. If you thrive under strict rules and micro-management, directed service requests are likely to be comfortable for you. If, however, you prefer more freedom in your service and would rather have the ability to choose methods and means of delivering service, a strictly directed service relationship will likely be frustrating for you.

Anticipatory Service

Anticipatory service comes from learning the habits and preferences the those we serve. Observation of those we serve can give us a plethora of information about their preferences, habits, and expectations. If you know your mistress gets thirsty after play and present her with a bottle of water without being asked, that is anticipatory service. Some dominants enjoy anticipatory service, others don't. If you are self-motivated, you'll likely enjoy anticipatory service more than you will directed service. I know that I prefer the freedom to meet the needs of those I serve without their directives rather than having to wait for them to tell me what to do.

Make sure you talk with your owner about the areas of their life in which anticipatory service is appropriate. I know that while the man I serve might appreciate having lunch brought to him if we've planned to do so, arriving at his place of work unannounced would be unacceptable behavior on my part. His work is inviolate and not an area of his life where I am permitted to enter without clear invitation. I know this because we've discussed the areas of his life where I am welcome to perform anticipatory services and those areas where I may only tread under directives from him. Take the time to clearly define such boundaries with your owner to avoid embarrassment or intrusive service.

Many consensual slavery relationships include a combination of directed and anticipatory service opportunities. On occasion, the man I serve will call me in the morning and give me a list of tasks to complete during the day. Often they relate to errands he doesn't have the time or inclination to complete. At the same time, I know that he expects my home to be clean and my dog to be cared for. These are all directed service opportunities. When poker night comes around and I ensure there is a bottle of his favorite beverage available at the location so I can pour him a drink as he sits down at the table, that is anticipatory service. I know he likes the beverage and enjoys having a drink with his friends as they play poker. He hasn't asked that the bottle be present, but appreciates when it is.

When you engage in a power exchange relationship, you'll likely find an ebb and flow of directed and anticipatory service opportunities. Early in the relationship, the dominant is likely to give many more directives than he or she might later in the relationship. Once you and your owner have spent more time together and have begun to learn each other's habits and preferences, the need for your owner to direct every service will lessen and you'll be confident enough in the relationship to begin offering anticipatory services more frequently. With positive feedback from your owner for the anticipatory services, you're likely to continue to complete them and expand your repertoire of anticipatory services to fit your owner's habits and needs.

As your relationship matures, you may find a shift in your responsibilities. Perhaps you now live with your owner and need to shift from the duties you performed at a distance to those which need to be completed in the home. Your owner may give your more directives to help you adjust to the new situation and to keep you informed of new responsibilities. Keeping the lines of communication open will help you both remain comfortable with the types of service you perform throughout your day and your relationship.

Intrusive Service

Intrusive service is any service which interrupts the flow of the dominant's activities. I once sat in on a workshop where the presenter's slave sat on the floor and constantly plucked the cuff of the man's ill-tailored pants off the top of his shoes. It was distracting and annoying to me as an audience member and caused the dominant to be constantly aware of where his slave was so he wouldn't step on her. Any service, whether it is directed or anticipatory, can be intrusive if it is performed in a manner that draws attention to the servant and interrupts the dominant as he or she is engaged with others or in other tasks.

It has always been a personal belief of mine that service should be unobtrusive. The glass at his hand should be full without the need for him to either ask or direct the contents. The daily tasks should be completed without constant input so that the owner's life is free of those distractions. Because of this belief, I find intrusive service contrary to my entire concept of servitude. I should be able to find ways to complete my services without interrupting what the owner is doing. And if I cannot, I need to discuss that with the owner. If my over-riding task as a servant is to make the life of those I serve easier and more comfortable, how does interrupting their day with my service meet that goal?

And if you think you might detect a little disdain for intrusive service in my tone, you'd be right. I have been in relationships where I was the home-keeper who created the comfortable home and met the goal of making the owner's life easier. There were others in that relationship who seemed to delight in countering everything I did to keep a calm home. Often it was through what I would consider intrusive service, including demanding recognition for every minor task completed, even when those tasks didn't meet minimum standards or were performed in such a manner as to completely disrupt what the owner was doing at the time. I cannot make choices for you or your partner as you structure your relationship, I can only tell you that my experiences with intrusive service have never been positive.

So much of what we do as servants is focused on helping our owners find peace in their lives. Intrusive service often makes dominants tense and uncomfortable (how would you feel should someone interrupt your life to do something they felt you needed to have done?). Such reactions are counter to what we try to accomplish for those we serve.

I recommend talking with your owner about the types of service and their preferences during your negotiations. If you discuss it and find that a prospective owner prefers to micro-manage your day, are you going to be happy in that type of relationship? If there are very few areas of the owner's life where you are going to be able to offer your service, will that wear on you or can you be happy? Taking the time to negotiate these things prior to engaging in a relationship may save you the frustration of being bound to service types you are unhappy with and unfulfilled by.

The Care and Feeding of a Slave

The chapters in this section of the book address issues and ideas which require your consideration if you are looking to become a successful consensual slave. Some chapters include exercises and recommended activities. Taking the time to complete those activities will give you valuable insight into yourself and your service.

What a Slave Needs

I've talked about the importance of differentiating between wants and needs prior to negotiating a power exchange relationship. While I cannot determine your personal needs, I can tell you that certain things are necessary to creating a successful power exchange relationship. Clearly defined boundaries and expectations, consistency, feedback and service opportunities are the foundation of any successful power exchange dynamic. Each of these areas will have individual differences based on the power exchange relationship dynamic in which the servant is engaged, but if one or more of these areas is neglected, issues will arise which would otherwise be avoidable.

Boundaries and Expectations

Have you ever watched a kitten explore a new environment? They creep along the edges, jump at every noise and smack anything that moves. They're finding their boundaries and testing the expectations of each object they encounter. A slave will often behave in a very similar manner when they enter into a power exchange relationship dynamic.

Until the boundaries of the relationship and the slave's role within the relationship are set, the slave will push at the perceived edges until the firm wall is found. To be successful in service, a slave needs to have those boundaries clearly defined at the beginning of the relationship. This will minimize the time and effort spent finding them on their own. Few things are more frustrating to a servant than to back into a wall they didn't know was there.

Along with boundaries and role definitions, a slave needs a solid understanding of the expectations the one they serve has for them. What are they to wear? How are they to speak? In what manner should they move? Additionally, slaves need a clear understanding of what they can and cannot expect from the dominant they serve. All of these boundaries and expectations should be a part of the relationship negotiations, but should also be evaluated from time to time to ensure the relationship is growing and remaining healthy.

With expectations must come a clear statement of the consequences that will follow should those expectations not be met. Expectations without consequences are just suggestions. If the slave fails to meet an expectation, what consequence will he or she face? Are those consequences appropriate to the degree of failure? Are the consequences consistently applied? The answers to these questions will help the slave and dominant structure their power exchange relationship dynamic to be healthy and happy for both of them. Failure to address expectations and consequences will severely hamper the servant's ability to remain balanced and comfortable in his or her station.

Consider the difference between a well-behaved child and a poorly-behaved child. Often the major difference between the two is that the well-behaved child knows the rules and the consequences of breaking those rules while the poorly-behaved child is constantly testing his or her boundaries and being surprised by the consequences of crossing lines they did not know where there. How often have you seen a submissive at a party acting out? Have you ever spoken to one; asked him or her why they behave in obviously inappropriate ways? My guess is part of their acting out stems from the failure of their power exchange relationship dynamic to clearly set forth boundaries, expectations, and consistently applied consequences.

Consistency

Once a slave understands his or her place in the power exchange relationship dynamic, the next need they have in order to be both happy and successful is the need for consistency. If an expectation has been laid out and a consequence noted for not meeting the expectation, that consequence should be consistently applied each time the expectation is not met. A failure to maintain consistency in the relationship dynamic will often lead a servant to feel the need to test boundaries again.

Inconsistency can lead to a thought process which goes something like this:

I was supposed to do A and didn't do it. He/She didn't notice or say anything so I guess I don't need to continue to do A.

Or worse yet:

He/She didn't notice or say anything so I guess what I'm doing isn't important.

I know it might seem childish, but I can tell you from experience how destructive inconsistency can be. While I don't need to be recognized each time I complete a task, (I am human and so occasionally attempt to get by with minimum requirements that barely meet standards) failure on the part of an owner to notice a failure on my part leaves me wondering if they notice anything I do. And if they don't notice what I do or don't do, why do I bother? It is at this point that communication with your owner becomes very important. If you feel your failures and your successes are going unnoticed, address it with your owner in the manner appropriate to your power exchange relationship.

As a slave, you hold significant responsibility for pointing out lapses in application of consequences. This is not to say a slave must always tattle on him or herself. We all do things we'd like to have overlooked from time to time. However, if the slave notices a consistent lack of application of consequences for not meeting certain expectations, it becomes his or her responsibility to approach the dominant, within the accepted boundaries of the relationship, and inquire as to whether a certain expectation is no longer valid.

It might seem counterproductive to point out that you haven't been meeting an expectation, but in truth, maintaining clear consequences for failure to meet expectations helps most servants retain their own mental stability and worth to the relationship. I know that were the one I serve to let me slide repeatedly on not meeting his expectations, I would begin to resent the times he *did* call me out for it. My thought process would be, "Why this time but not that time?"

Now realistically, there is nothing wrong with changing what is expected so long as that change is shared with the servant. If a dominant really doesn't care about having his or her slippers warmed in the morning, they shouldn't make that an expectation. If they have made warming their slippers in the morning an expectation and it is not done, it is the dominant's responsibility to either apply correction or remove the expectation. Failure to do one of those two things will leave the servant in a position to question their usefulness to the dominant and to question the other expectations set forth in the power exchange dynamic.

Consistency from the dominant in nearly any aspect of a power exchange relationship dynamic can be a true rock to which a servant can cling for stability and happiness. Without it, the dominant may suddenly find themselves in possession of a disobedient brat, when they had originally negotiated a relationship with an obedient slave.

It is important to note that the servant has just as much responsibility toward ensuring consistency in the relationship as the owner does. As a consensual slave, you should feel a certain obligation to your owner to tell them about transgressions when you know they won't discover them. You should feel enough pride in your service to want to maintain your personal integrity by ensuring you keep your owner informed of everything that will affect them and your service to them.

Feedback

I don't know if it is part of the submissive nature or if it is just that often those who identify as submissive are also extrinsically motivated people, but I've noticed that many of us on the "s" side of M/s and D/s relationships need feedback and acknowledgement from those we serve in order to maintain a happy outlook and continue to be productive members of power exchange relationships.

The inherent problem with this particular need is that often what we do as servants goes without notice or comment. How often have you simply refilled a glass, picked up clothing from the cleaners, or cleaned a playspace without comment from those you serve? How can a servant continue to feel valued if feedback and acknowledgement are not forthcoming? It is up to the servant to find ways to be intrinsically motivated in their service to remove some of that need from the relationship.

Now I am not, by any stretch, saying that servants shouldn't be thanked for what they do or that they should allow themselves to be taken advantage of in any relationship. What I am saying is that finding a way to be internally motivated to serve—finding what it is inside ourselves that makes service pleasurable for us—will remove the burden of constant acknowledgement and feedback from those we serve and allow our service to become more natural and free-flowing. Can we truly be effective in service if we feel the need to wait for acknowledgement or feedback after each task?

Personally, I have found that completing service tasks is pleasurable because I like to see things "become." When I clean, the pleasure of seeing a room transformed from the disheveled mess to the neat, functional space is equal to any pleasure I might feel if those I serve were to acknowledge that I cleaned the room. Additionally, I cannot imagine the disruption to my personal flow (what I do on a day to day basis—I'm a very structure and schedule type person) waiting for acknowledgement would create.

Making the switch to intrinsic motivation does not mean you are forbidden from asking for feedback from those you serve if you are unsure about your performance in a given area. After the first time I attended a largish lifestyle event with the man I was in service to at the time, I asked for specific feedback on my performance because there had been areas in which I felt I did not meet his standards and expectations. Asking for constructive criticism of service is not the same as pointing out each service you perform. Requesting constructive criticism demonstrates your willingness to improve. Pointing out each service you perform and asking for acknowledgement of that service will often negate the value of said service as you pat yourself on the back rather than allowing your service to speak for itself. Consider this—if you must point out how well you performed a service, do you really believe that service was up to standard? And if you point out each service, are you not removing the right to praise or criticize from those you serve?

Learning to make the shift from extrinsic to intrinsic motivation often begins with assessing why you might seek out approval and motivation from others. Do you do so because you feel inadequate or lack confidence? If so, you must address these issues personally and consider your overall motivations for being involved in a power exchange relationship. If you seek approval to make up for low self-esteem, who are you really serving?

Finding intrinsic motivation for service does not eliminate all need for feedback or acknowledgement, but it does mitigate it. There is an additional bonus inherent in a shift from extrinsic to intrinsic motivation as well. When you have completed a service and have gained your intrinsic value from it, you may still receive acknowledgement and feedback from those you serve. There is little in the life of a servant which compares to hearing, "Good job," from those we serve, especially when that praise comes without prompting from us.

Consider Your Motivations

This is a good time to stop and consider your own motivations for service. Make a list of services you provide or wish to provide for an owner and then consider what motivates your desire to perform those services. For example, perhaps you wish to cook for an owner. Are you motivated by a love of cooking, a desire to care for the nutritional needs of your owner or something else?

Understanding why you serve will help you serve more comfortably and make it possible for you to offer more and better service to your owner.

Service Opportunities

It almost seems superfluous to mention the need for service opportunities in a discussion about slaves and servants, but in truth, the opportunity to serve is paramount to the health and well-being of a servant.

Believe it or not, servants do understand the need dominants have to do things for themselves. However, if a dominant has set forth a particular service for the servant to perform on a regular basis, it is best for the dominant to try not to take that from them without explanation. Doing so sets off a self-destructive train of thought in the minds of many servants. "Why did he do that? I'm supposed to do that. I must not be doing it right if he's doing it for himself."

This need to serve can be further complicated by the introduction of other servants into a polyamorous family. As the slave, it is your responsibility to speak up for yourself. Include the need for service opportunities in your negotiations. Use your free speech times to address issues of service with your dominant. I know that when I negotiated my current relationship, I specifically requested that should others be brought in to serve him, they not be given a task that was previously mine without telling me first. I know, from hard experience, that I can be rather proprietary about the tasks I perform for those I serve. I also know that when such tasks are taken from me without warning, I can lose focus and balance and begin to doubt myself and my skills.

My request does not put any restrictions on the owner other than requesting that I be kept informed. His agreement to that portion of our negotiation simply means that should another servant be given a task that was previously mine, I would be informed. I feel such an arrangement is fair and once I explained the purpose behind it, so did the man I now serve. It might be unseemly for a servant to admit to being proprietary over services performed, but the truth is that such feelings are part of a servant's humanity. When we do something well and repeatedly, taking it from us without warning and giving it to another servant is cause for mental and emotional distress. If you know yourself well enough that removal of certain services from your responsibility will have this type of affect on you, make sure to address it with your owner.

Having defined or even spur of the moment service opportunities available to a servant will also help servants shift from directed to anticipatory services. If, for example, a dominant tells you to get him or her a drink, that is directed service. If the next time the dominant reaches for a drink and it is there because you noticed the glass was empty and refilled it, you have performed an anticipatory service. With positive feedback for your anticipatory service, you'll likely continue to perform it.

If, however, you interrupt the one you serve to ask if she's thirsty and then run through the gamut of options, all the while keeping her from returning to what she was doing before you interrupted, you are being intrusive. If there are regular service opportunities built into the relationship, the need to interrupt to request such opportunities is reduced. Busy servants are usually happy servants. Bored servants, because they wish to be useful, may become intrusive in their quest for service opportunities.

An argument can even be made that any service is intrusive if it is not part of the pre-defined service opportunities set forth in the power exchange dynamic. As such, it is important to know what areas of the dominant's life you are welcome, and which are off limits. If those boundaries are clear, creating service opportunities becomes a positive exercise for both the servant and the served.

Regardless of your own relationship dynamic, remember that the people engaged in the relationship are human and have their own wants, needs and desires. While many wants and desires of servants can be set aside in a power exchange relationship dynamic, needs such as those discussed here are actually central to the overall success of the power exchange relationship dynamic. Failure to consider and then define these areas may ultimately result in the failure of the power exchange relationship dynamic. As the servant, your responsibility for negotiating these needs into your relationship is immense, and may seem out of proportion to the responsibilities of the dominant. But remember, it is your happiness at stake, and no one ever said life was fair.

Preparing for Life as a Consensual Slave

One thing you always need to remember when you are either considering or living a life of consensual slavery is that no matter what else you are, you are human. Sometimes we servants forget that we aren't supermen and women. We are mere mortals with all the foibles of our mortal selves. We get sick. We have our hearts broken. We move to new homes. We do everything everyone else does, but we do it all with the knowledge and acknowledgement that we serve another.

I can't tell you how many times I've had people come to me and say, "How do you do it all? I can barely keep my own life in order, let alone anyone else's." The truth is, sometimes I don't do it all. All to often I am faced with my own human limitations and how they interact with my service. I'm going to make several suggestions in this chapter which I believe are valuable whether you are already engaged in a power exchange relationship or not. I hope you'll take some time and complete these exercises because I know how valuable the information can be to you. This chapter will address self-assessment, coping mechanisms and the pitfalls of being totally immersed in the leather lifestyle.

Self-Assessment

I strongly recommend taking the time to do a fair amount of self-assessment prior to engaging in a power exchange relationship. The self-assessment can be formalized, such as completing a personality test, or a more casual assessment of your strengths and weaknesses. Either way (and I honestly recommend doing both), this process is going to take some time. Don't rush your self-assessment and take time to go back and re-assess periodically. And I caution you to be brutally honest with yourself. I know how hard it can be to admit to your faults, but failure to do so will invalidate so much of the self-assessment process. Bite the bullet, admit your faults, and find ways to make them work for you.

Personality tests can be helpful in gaining initial insight into your personality type. There are many free tests available online and a Google search will put you in touch with many of them. I recommend some variation of the Myers-Briggs typological test, as it seems to be the most comprehensive. These tests look at four areas of your personality and gauge your response on a continuum between pairs of traits.

The information gained from these tests may surprise you. Often the explanations of the personality types are eerily accurate. For example, I completed the test found on the Humanmetrics website and it concluded that I was an ISFJ (Introvert, Sensing, Feeling, Judging).

According to Keirsey (n.d) "The primary desire of (ISFJ) is to be of service to others, but here, 'service' means not so much furnishing others with the necessities of life...,as guarding others against life's pitfalls and perils, that is, seeing to their safety and security." Anyone who has met me can tell you that the Keirsey description fits me to a "T". Later in the description, it even mentions the perceived coldness others feel when first meeting an ISFJ (something I've struggled with all my life). Marina Margaret Heiss (2007) includes in her description of the ISFJ traits such as unwillingness to engage in confrontation and a tendency to put their own concerns on the back-burner to keep from "burdening others" with their problems.

Seeing these traits in writing and knowing they apply to nearly ten percent of the population (Keirsey, n.d.), makes it easier to see how my day-to-day reactions to stimuli might be affected by my personality. I know that given a choice, I will stick to the edges of a party and observe until I feel comfortable. Often I am perceived as being cold and uncaring when in fact I am simply watching and learning before I venture into the fray. My friends and family will tell you that should you be willing to get past the distance I place between myself and the rest of the world, you'll find someone warm and loving and loyal to a fault.

It is also helpful to share this information with your prospective or current owner. If your owner understands, as mine does, that you will serve him to the detriment of yourself, he or she can be on the look out for physical and emotional indications that you are reaching your limit.

Personality tests like the Meyers-Briggs test can also help you determine what your strengths and weaknesses are. The evaluation and explanation of your personality type will likely point to several places of strength and weakness in your personality. In my case, I've always been aware that I am not good at confrontation. I will do everything in my power to avoid confrontation, even if it means damaging myself. On the positive side, I'm loyal to those I care about. Although I have to admit that I've been known to take even loyalty too far. I have trouble letting go of people I care about, even when keeping them in my life is detrimental.

Take time to complete one of these tests and then analyze the results as they apply specifically to your life and personality. Use the results to analyze your strengths and weaknesses, and then share what you've learned with your owner. The better you know yourself, the better able you are to meet the challenges of being a consensual slave.

I also recommend that part of your self-assessment include an analysis of your triggers. Perhaps you know that you are easily upset by public humiliation. Maybe overt sexual activity in front of others sets you off. Whatever your triggers are, be aware of them and be sure to share them with your owner. Now, do understand that depending on the negotiated relationship you have with your owner, he or she may use those triggers against you, but you should still share them. No one likes to be ambushed by a problem they didn't know existed. Sharing your triggers with your owner gives them the opportunity to prepare should a trigger be hit upon or purposely pushed as part of play.

For example, I know that high stress situations will cause me to retreat into a facade of the disciplined and emotionally detached servant. During the protocol dinner held at APEX in May of 2006, I had done just that. I was the efficient, silent servant going through each task and ensuring the dominants in attendance were well cared for. When I violated a rule during the dinner, I was punished for it and retreated even further into the facade. Because the man I served at the time wanted more of a reaction from me than he got from the punishment, he turned to pushing triggers I had shared with him about public humiliation. The end result was me in tears and him embarrassed because he'd pushed one trigger too many. My attempt to mitigate my stress throughout the day by hiding behind my strengths left him in a position where better communication on my part might have saved both of us embarrassment.

Be brutally honest in your self-evaluation. Don't hold anything back when you're looking at yourself or when you're sharing your findings with your owner. If you have behavior patterns you revert to in certain situations, tell your owner so they can watch for the warning signs. If you keep this information from them, you are removing their ability to make decisions from a position of full disclosure and you place them in an uncomfortable position of having to deal with you after you've lost it and everyone else who witnessed the disintegration of a normally well-behaved servant.

Coping Mechanisms

Being a consensual slave can be both fulfilling and exhausting. Sometimes the strictures of these relationships can be overwhelming and we need to find outlets for our human emotions and reactions. Generally speaking (and I say this from the experience of several total power exchange relationships), screaming obscenities at your owner is not an acceptable outlet for frustration or anger.

I've found writing to be a great coping mechanism. Often just writing down the horrible, ugly things I'm thinking is enough to get rid of them. I need never share those words, but dumping them helps me feel better. Writing about the good things helps too. It gives you an opportunity to go back and relive the best parts of your life. I know many power exchange relationships in which a daily diary is a requirement for the servant. While I agree that writing and sometimes sharing that writing is good for the soul, I also know that writing every day isn't always productive. I often go months without anything to write in a personal journal. Forcing me to write when I have nothing to say is actually counter-productive for me. I'd rather write nothing than make something up to fulfill an arbitrary requirement.

I'm also not a fan of every single word needing to be shared. If I am using writing as a coping mechanism and a way to get rid of what I feel are destructive thoughts, sharing them after the fact may not be helpful to either me or the relationship. Sometimes I just need to scream "Mother Fucker" at the top of my lungs. I don't need anyone to hear me scream for that to make me feel better. The same goes for writing out the hurt or anger of something trivial that means nothing by the time I get the words out of my head and onto paper.

Sometimes it's a good idea to find a fellow servant to talk to. Humans connect with others who have similar experiences, making it easier to cope when you can get confirmation that what you feel is entirely normal. I do caution you to choose such a confidant carefully. The local gossip is likely not a good choice for such conversations, unless you want your personal life bandied about. I also don't recommend talking over service issues with dominants other than the one you serve. Doing so can set up a "he said, she said" situation which can be far more damaging than holding your tongue.

Most dominants I've known in the community encourage their servants to find other servants to talk with. They recognize the human necessity of sharing experiences and know that they don't always have the right answers for their servants. Serving and being served are completely different life experiences and the two don't always understand each other as one on the same path would.

If you have hobbies and interests, keep up with them. If you don't you'll begin to resent your owner and any perceived force on their part which keeps you from the things you enjoy. An added benefit to maintaining your hobbies is that doing things we enjoy reduces our stress levels and gives us an outlet for emotions which might be inappropriate in our power exchange relationship. If your interests include physical activities like martial arts or working out, stick with them. Your body and your soul will thank you, as will your owner when presented with a more balanced and happy servant.

Pitfalls of Immersion

Sometimes we find ourselves completely immersed in the Leather Community and while there are some advantages to immersion, the truth is there are far more pitfalls than advantages. I've lived the last two years of my life completely immersed in the Leather Community and so I speak from experience here when I tell you, find outside interests to keep yourself balanced and happy.

For nine months, I lived in a literal 24/7 total power exchange relationship. I also helped to run several lifestyle businesses. The man I served and I rarely did anything outside the community. It was both wonderful and awful at the same time.

The isolation of being completely immersed in the Leather Community like that can wear on a servant very quickly. If you are constantly on when it comes to public protocol and aware that everything you do and say is being judged by the community, you can quickly become tired and edgy. I also found myself separating from more vanilla pursuits and having to find ways to explain my extensively busy schedule to vanilla friends and family. In short, it was exhausting.

I strongly recommend using the coping mechanisms discussed above to help you maintain a balanced mental outlook. But I also suggest finding vanilla pursuits to keep yourself centered in the vanilla world as well. As wonderful as the Leather Community can be, total immersion in it can easily drain the life and enjoyment of service from the most dedicated servant.

Choosing to live as a consensual slave is a life-altering choice that no one can make for you. One of the main reasons I've written this book is to help those who are considering such a life understand that it won't be like Robin in *The Slave*. As much as I enjoy that book and might wish for such a life, the Marketplace doesn't exist and Chris Parker isn't going to take me into his home and train me personally[33]. Taking time to prepare yourself for life as a consensual slave will help you find the areas of your life which may not be conducive to a power exchange relationship and give you the time and tools to decide if making changes in your life or deciding not to journey down this path is the right choice for you. I hope you will use the tools I've provided and complete the tasks I've suggested before you jump into a consensual slavery relationship. I'd be willing to bet that if you do, you'll be happier either as a consensual slave or by finding out the life is not for you.

Heiss , M (2007, Aug 20). Introverted Sensing Feeling Judging. Retrieved November 4, 2007, from Typelogic Web site: http://typelogic.com/isfj.html

Keirsey temperament website: The four temperaments. Retrieved November 4, 2007, from Keirsey.com Web site: http://keirsey.com/handler.aspx?s=keirsey&f=fourtemps&tab=2&c=protector

---

[33] *The Slave* is the second book of *The Marketplace Series*. Robin is the main character of the book and is included in later books as well. She is chosen by Chris Parker, a recurring character who trains the slaves for The Marketplace, for private training in preparation for an auction. Robin's training, while similar to the training received by other Marketplace slaves, differs because she receives one-on-one time and attention from Parker. Many consensual slaves who read *The Slave* express a desire to be trained in a manner similar to Robin.

Humanity and the Power Exchange Relationship

No matter the details of a power exchange relationship, regardless of the particular protocols observed by the servants and expected by the owners, power exchange relationships are relationships between and among human beings. As such, there are human foibles and problems that will arise during the course of the relationship. Acknowledging that humans are involved and being willing to work out those human issues will help you build relationships that are more successful.

The Humanity of Slaves

Sometimes slaves are so efficient that those they serve forget they're human too. I know there have been times in my life when the man I was in service to continued to give me tasks long after I was physically able to complete them. My drive to be perfect and complete any task given to me caused me to push myself past breaking. At that point, I would have a complete break-down, crying and freaking out, only to be told by the owner that I should have spoken up. He knew I couldn't finish everything and had been waiting for me to admit it as well.

Generally, I've found that if my needs are being met, some of my wants are granted and I am given leave to adjust my priorities when my vanilla life requires more of my attention, I can be both successful and happy, able to give my all to what the owner needs from me. If, however, any of those three things are not met, I get downright bitchy and bratty in an effort to demonstrate my inability to keep up. I know I have trouble speaking up when I'm feeling overwhelmed. Because I know this about myself, I am sure to share that fact with anyone I serve in the hope they'll help me when I reach the breaking point.

That is not to say that I am giving up on my own responsibility to speak up and tell the owner that I simply cannot continue. Instead, I know I have trouble saying "no" (especially to the owner) and so I will often ask, instead for permission to be told "no."[34] A common refrain from the man I now serve is, "I don't give you enough to do, do I?" The truth is, serving him is pretty mild compared to the mounds of work my previous relationships amounted to. The current owner is a self-sufficient, professional man who doesn't really need me to micromanage any portion of his life, so I'm left with a lot more free time than I might like. I get bored easily. When he does give me tasks to complete, I will immerse myself in them until they are complete. Asking for permission to be told no is a simple as saying to him, "Sir, I've been asked to do xyz. I have abc to complete first. What should I do." Because the owner knows, from my admission to him, of my tendency to accept more than I can handle, he can tell me at this point, "No, you may not do xyz."

The owner wants a happy and healthy servant, and yours will too. Sharing your human weaknesses and agreeing upon things such as my need to ask permission to be told no, will help you both reach that goal. Don't think you have no responsibility when it comes to this area of your life. You accepted responsibility for it when you shared your habits with your owner and arranged for ways for him or her to help you to be healthy. I recommend talking to your owner when you feel overwhelmed. Your owner chose you because you had traits he or she found attractive. They will want to know when you feel you cannot meet their expectations, rather than facing the explosion when you've reached your wits end. Do not take from your owner their right to care for their property by hiding the fact you feel overwhelmed. Give them enough information so they can care for their property and maintain a useful servant.

One of the chapters in this book is about self-assessment. I strongly recommend completing the tasks set forth in that chapter, not just because it's good to know yourself, but also because if you have facts and information to share with your owner, you make it easier for them to be merciful. I cannot imagine any conscientious owner purposely setting out to destroy their property. I can't tell you how many times those I serve

---

[34] Because I have so much trouble telling anyone that I cannot do what they have asked of me, I sometimes turn to the owner for help in saying no. Rather than just telling someone, "No, I can't do that," asking for permission to be told no means I can say, "I'm sorry, but the owner said I can't do that for you." In essence, asking for permission to be told no means the owner tells me I cannot say yes and I in turn can feel I have support from him for saying no to the other person. It may seem weak of me to need his support in something like this, but I am lucky enough that the man I server understands me well enough to offer me this kind of support.

have told me that "broken toys are no fun." If that is the case, that your owner doesn't want broken property, why would you break their property for them? If you know enough about yourself and your triggers and you share that information with your owner, you are giving them the opportunity to offer assistance before you reach critical mass.

I know how hard it can be for a servant to speak up and say, "I can't do that, Sir." I've been there, I promise. We want so much to give those we serve everything they want and need. But we have to recognize our own human limitations and ensure we are not usurping our owner's rights to take burdens from us. Hard though it may be, when we agreed to engage in a total power exchange relationship, we gave all of ourselves to our owners, and that includes our humanity. Let your owner see you are human and let them decide to relieve your burdens rather than suffering in silence.

And just as the vanilla world will drag us kicking and screaming out of the dungeon, sometimes vanilla priorities will take us away from our service. I know that should my family need me, the man I serve would gladly give me up for the time they needed me because he understands how important my parents are in my life. When your vanilla life priorities become a burden or begin to infringe on time in service to your owner, talk to them. Most owners I've known willingly work with their servants to help them balance their vanilla priorities with their service priorities. Again, keeping the lines of communication open will help you both when issues like this arise.

The Humanity of Owners

This might come as a surprise to you, but owners are human too. I know we sometimes build our owners up as Gods and Goddesses with no flaws. But reality must step in and remind us that our owners have the same doubts and problems as we do.

Owners will make mistakes. Yes, really. They aren't always right. As servants, sometimes our job is to allow our owners to save face by not pointing out their flaws, but rather serving them in ways which help them be successful in spite of them.

Owners have vanilla priorities as well, priorities that may take them away from you and their ownership of you. It is our job as servants to help our owners with their vanilla priorities (when it is appropriate) so they can pursue other interests. You might be surprised how much help doing the laundry, or cooking meals can be when your owner has heavy vanilla pressures in his or her life. As much as it is appropriate, be aware of what is going on in your owner's life and look for ways you can help them. Learn their habits and quirks and take note of what their stressors are. The more you can ease their stress in one area of their life, the more they are able to handle the rest. I know when I hear stress in the owner's voice after a long day at work, I can ease him with just the offer of care.

It is here that learning and using your owner's preferences becomes important. The more you know about your owner, the better able you will be to ease their lives in times of stress. The less stress you bring to them, the better. That is not to say you should hide your stress from them. I've learned from hard experience that doing so often causes more problems than sharing the stress would have in the first place. Instead, use your service as a way to alleviate stress from other areas of your owners life by meeting their expectations.

It is important to recognize those times when you owner may need nothing more than to be left to themselves. Part of the humanity of owners is their egos, something we all have but which seem to grow to monstrous proportions in those who identify as dominant. If your owner has suffered a blow to his or her ego, the last thing they may want is your presence to observe what they feel is an embarrassment. Respect their right to save face and walk away. I even recommend looking at a situation and deciding if your presence would embarrass your owner without their input.

I will often stay back when I arrive at a location after the owner has. I don't immediately reach for him or display affection until I am certain it is appropriate. He tells me it is appropriate by reaching for me (or grabbing me as I attempt to walk past to put the beer in the fridge while he's playing pool) and either asking for, or taking the mode of affection he wants. Our relationship is such that certain circumstances require more distance between us than others. Giving him that space rather than pouncing on him when I arrive, or when he arrives after I do, allows him to maintain his dignity and to set the tone at his comfort level. The ego of a dominant can be so fragile. Allowing them to make decisions about how to protect it will help you keep them comfortable even in uncomfortable situations.

For example, when the man I serve decided he wished to learn a new whip throw, he knew he was going to smack himself repeatedly in the process of learning the throw and told me I was not to watch. I respected his wishes and left the dungeon so he could learn without the pressure of being "The Owner" where I could see him in a less than dignified manner. Giving him space to be human rather than making it necessary that he remain "The Owner," is important to the health of our relationship.

Gauging when your owner requires space and when they do not is part of knowing the real person with whom you are involved. Remember the fantasy versus reality discussion earlier in this book? Once you know the person better than you know the fantasy, you'll be better able to determine when you need to step back and when you should step forward. Not all owners are uncomfortable about appearing less than dignified. Not all situations with the same owner will require the same reaction from the servant. The man I serve is not shy about being silly and behaving in a manner that is anything but dignified. The fact that he is this way makes me much quicker to accept his need for me to step away if he feels he will be embarrassed. I've seen him be silly. I've seen him hurt himself. I've seen him do things he wished I would have missed and he is not diminished in my eyes. But if he wishes me to leave rather than witness what he knows will be uncomfortable, I am happy to oblige.

It is important for the participants in any relationship, power exchange or not, to be cognizant of the pressures of humanity as they fall on the partners. Take time to find methods of countering those pressures, both for yourself and for your owner, and you'll find that your relationship is healthier than should you simply let the pressures build to explosion.

When Your Play Styles Don't Match

The majority of the chapters in this book deal with relationship issues outside the playroom. The playroom or dungeon, however, can play a significant role in the happiness of your power exchange relationship. So what happens when you meet the person you want to serve but they like to play in ways you would normally avoid? Is this a deal-breaking issue for you? Can you learn to like what they enjoy? Are you willing to accept what they like for the sake of obedience? Can you be happy if they want to play with others? Only you can answer these questions, but be prepared to do so should the situation arise.

And while the examples I use mirror my own experiences as a non-masochist slave in service to a sadist, other permutations of top/bottom dynamics exist in our community. What if the one you serve comes to you, crop in hand, and says, "Beat me until I cry?" Could you do that? Would you obey the directive or fail to do so because the thought of hitting him or her has you on the verge of hysterics?

Clear negotiation of needs and wants on the part of the dominant in the relationship prior to engaging in the total power exchange should head off situations such as this, but we servants know how hard it can be to get our owners (or prospective) owners to open up to us about their needs and wants.

Having once been in a position to inflict pain on a former owner during an auction, I found that I am incapable of hurting those I serve or have served. And it isn't just that at one time I couldn't imagine hurting anyone. I no longer feel that way. If I can beat someone with a flogger tipped with Exacto blades or cut them with scalpels or dance with them and a single-tail, I can hurt people. I just cannot hurt those to whom I have surrendered. Knowing this about myself would mean should the owner come to me and say, "Beat me until I cry," I would be unable to obey without doing some serious damage to my mental state. Top that off with my inability to even watch others hurt those to whom I have surrendered and you have a servant who would flee the dungeon should the owner choose to engage in a cathartic beating.

Communication and negotiation should keep you and your owner out of these uncomfortable situations. I have shared not only my feelings on the matter with the man I now serve, but also the stories of having been in such situations. He respects my feelings on the matter and appreciates my honesty. The fact that hell would likely freeze over before the owner bottomed to anyone helps too.

I am not a masochist. I don't enjoy pain. I'm unable to process pain into pleasure. If you hit me, I'll cry, and that crying will be real for the time it continues. The man I serve (and basically every other I have served in the past) is a sadist. He enjoys inflicting pain in various ways and using different methods. He is, more specifically, a sexual sadist who is sexually aroused by hurting someone who is not always enjoying the pain. So why do I choose to serve men like this?

The answer to that question is complicated. I choose those I serve based on many things, play style being fairly far down the priority list. Is he trustworthy? Is he willing and able to accept my service? Is he happy to negotiate and meet my needs as I meet his? Those are far more important questions than, "Do I like what he does to me in the dungeon?"

Suffering for and at the hands of the man I serve fulfills a service need for me. He knows I don't enjoy being whipped. Because he knows that, my willingness to obey without hesitation when he calls me into the dungeon is fulfilling to him as well. Ruthless obedience is, in the words of a good friend, "Sexy as hell." The man I serve agrees.

That being said, there are still internal conflicts that must be worked out when the play styles of the dominant and slave don't match up. There are a couple of ways to approach this issue.

The first is to find someone outside the relationship to play with the owner while the servant steps aside for play time. Should you choose this option with your partner, I'd like to make a few suggestions.

First, since the addition of anyone to a relationship, regardless of role, sets up a polyamorous relationship, be sure you are comfortable with the concept. I strongly recommend clearly defining the role of the player in the over-all relationship so no one is surprised about his or her appropriate place in the grand scheme of things.

Second, be prepared (as much as you can be) for emotional landmines. Servants sometimes become proprietary over the services they provide. Are you going to be able to watch your partner play with another? If so, what happens when play leads to other intimacies? Addressing these issues internally and then discussing them with your partner can head off some very volatile situations.

Finally, communicate. You'll see me repeat this mantra throughout my writing. Servants are human. Sometimes we agree to something because we honestly believe what we say, but find out later we're emotionally or physically unable to complete our task. Those we serve are human as well and would rather hear our concerns than deal with broken property as a result of us withholding information.

Another option is to find ways to incorporate into your play time things both players enjoy. If the slave enjoys flogging but the master prefers spanking, perhaps an agreement might be made that every so often, the master will flog the slave so he or she can enjoy a scene. Humans are much more likely to accept things they don't like if they are getting something they do like out of the bargain.

Agreeing to compromise like this does not constitute topping from the bottom[35] either. Consenting adults playing sadomasochistic games for their mutual pleasure and gratification should be willing to discuss likes and dislikes and be willing to "give to get." If repeatedly banging your head against the wall did nothing but give you a headache, you'd stop doing it, wouldn't you? Why should a sexual encounter that is entirely unsatisfactory for one person be repeated without variance?

Of course, the slave can simply do as he or she is told and accept the play as the master offers it. If this is the dynamic a power exchange relationship is built on, it is important for negotiations to include topics such as dealing with resentment, pain, and aftercare. This type of arrangement is fragile at times and requires an open dialogue between the servant and the master. Tread carefully if you choose this path and be

---

[35] Topping from the bottom is a phrase used to describe controlling behavior exhibited by slaves, submissives and bottoms. When a submissive dictates the method, means, and process of the relationship or scene, it is considered topping from the bottom.

ready for unexpected land mines to explode when you least expect them to. That being said, this arrangement can be successful and fulfilling for both partners if both are willing to work at it. The slave must be willing to find ways to process pain and emotional issues. The master must be willing to work with the slave as they find these methods.

As a slave who is not a masochist, I can share my experience and mindset but I cannot make a choice for you as to what type of relationship you should have. I am often conflicted about playing. That conflict is nothing new. I have felt it from the moment I found the Leather Community seven years ago, so I know it is not directed specifically at the relationship I am currently engaged in.

The conflict comes from hating to be hit, but feeling resentful if the man I serve doesn't play with me. I know, how can that possibly be a healthy way to feel about someone? The truth is, I don't resent him. Instead I feel somewhat inadequate for not liking what he likes. I feel guilty that he feels he must hold back from playing as he wants to because he's afraid of scaring me off. I feel as though I am failing in service because I cannot be what he wants...a heavy masochist who will beg him to hurt her.

I know that these feelings are mine and not his. We talk about this on a regular basis in order to remain connected and on the same page regarding these issues. I've learned some techniques for transferring pain. I recognize when I'm pushed too far and luckily he's tuned in to me well enough to do the same. The fact that he has medical training and watches my body's response to stimuli makes an enormous difference in our ability to communicate non-verbally during a scene. And we have agreed that he will stay with me following a scene until I am reconnected to myself and to him.

I often complicate the issue by attempting to remain obedient. Let me explain. If I am being hit with something that hurts, fight or flight[36] should make me move out of the path, right? Ruthless obedience leaves me not only in the position to continue to be hit, but tense and perhaps making it

---

[36] The "fight or flight response" is our body's primitive, automatic, inborn response that prepares the body to "fight" or "flee" from perceived attack, harm or threat to our survival.
Neimark, December 26, 2007 The fight or flight response. from Mind/Body Education Center Web site: http://www.thebodysoulconnection.com/EducationCenter/fight.html

easier to reach me. I will often attempt to be stoic and remain accessible to the owner long after my body has said, "Enough, idiot. That hurts." Just the other day, he bit me (something I generally enjoy) but did so in such a way that 1) it really hurt and 2) it pushed emotional buttons as it was done in a stressful situation. Tensing up, of course, made it worse (ever clenched your jaw while someone's teeth were locked on your cheek?). And crying made it worse because I had spent the evening fighting off tears for an unrelated reason. But I accepted the activity because he wanted it and when he asked if poking it hurt, I was honest and said no. So much of sadomasochistic play is more emotional than physical for me that it makes it very difficult for me to help my partners understand what's going on behind the tears. Only with continuing communication can a situation like this result in positive outcomes. Believe me, the laughter echoing through the parking lot later was a clear indication of how I felt about the evening as a whole.

To me, there often seems to be two different people to whom I belong. There is the loving man I serve day to day who knows me well enough to hear a change in my breathing and know something is either right or wrong. This is the man whose face fills my dreams when he isn't with me and whose arms hold me tight when he is. The other man is faceless. He is the sadist who reaches out of the dark and hurts me in ways I never imagined I would or could hurt. It is this faceless man who makes my heart thump as though I'm going to die, and who makes my hands reach for help when I would normally stand relaxed. It is the faceless man who makes me cry.

Because my brain literally sees two men in the man I serve, reconnection during and after a scene is paramount to my ability to stay balanced. He's told me many times, "How can I hurt you if I can't comfort you?". His willingness to hold me until the tears stop, to smile at me and regain his face, is what makes me able to be happy with the differences in what we like in the dungeon.

And I'm not the only one who is conflicted. He has told me how my tears affect him, while at the same time bragging that one of the sexiest things I've ever said was "If you hit me, I'll cry. I don't like pain, but if I'm yours I will let you hurt me." These issues are part of the necessary ongoing negotiation of our relationship.

Just the other day, he said to me, "You don't like pain, remember?" after I told him I'd been working out ways to resist him in the dungeon because he'd told me that was something he needed. He also told me he didn't want to break his favorite toy, so he doesn't play at full throttle with me. I'm conflicted by this. On the one hand it's wonderful to know he loves me enough to worry that unleashing his demons would cause me irreparable harm. On the other hand, the servant in me feels like a failure because I can't give him what he needs. Ultimately though, I am his to do with as he pleases. It is comforting to know he values me as much as he does.

Which is not to say he doesn't look for new and exquisite ways to push my buttons. He has told me that my ruthless obedience, even when he can read my displeasure on my face and in my body language, is fulfilling to him. In the next breath he told me he was still looking for ways to make me say "no." As a non-masochist, that can be scary. As a dedicated consensual slave, it's both comforting and exciting. I haven't said "no" yet and thankfully, I haven't come up with a reason why I would (my mind isn't quite as devious as his in that way). But knowing he's still interested in finding that last wall is hot.

It isn't easy when a sadist and a massawussy join forces, but who said any relationship should be easy? In my case, I serve him because I find service of any kind fulfilling, even service I don't like. No one ever said being a consensual slave was all fun and games. It is work and sometimes involves doing things you might otherwise never do. But so long as you are fulfilled by that work, you'll be happy as a consensual slave.

When Life Intrudes

Despite the fact that your desire to be a consensual slave might seem to be the single most important thing in your life, you have to be honest and recognize that life will intrude upon your desires. The chapters in this section will help you find a balance between service and vanilla responsibilities.

Organization and Time Management

Some of the most valuable skills you can learn on your path to becoming a consensual slave are those of organization and time management. I know that the rest of this book dealt mainly with relationship concepts, but the ability to remain organized and to carefully manage your time will make you a highly valuable slave and one who has time for the relationship "stuff." If you're already pretty organized and manage your time wisely, my hat is off to you! I know it is a struggle sometimes to remain focused and not waste an entire day doing nothing but wandering from one task to the next without actually accomplishing anything. This chapter will give you some ideas of how to get better organized and stay on task by managing your time better.

Using Activity Logs

Activity logs are exactly what they sound like. They are simple lists of what you do, how long it takes to do it, and of what value to your day that activity is. An excellent template can be downloaded for free from Mindtools[37].

Activity logs are designed to help us discover the "missing" time in our days. Have you ever said, "I'd be able to get everything done if I only had an extra hour each day?" I know I have. The truth is, that hour is likely somewhere in our day being wasted on a task or lack of task that contains no value to our goals. To find out where your missing hour is, get an activity log, like the one above, and commit to using it for one week.

Each time you do something, mark it down. Each time you change tasks, note the time. At the end of the week, go through your logs and mark each task with a value based on what that task accomplished for you and your goals. I'm willing to bet you'll find an extra hour or two a day where you weren't engaged in valuable tasks and that re-allotting that time will make your day run more smoothly.

---

[37] http://www.mindtools.com/pages/article/worksheets/ActivityLogDownload.htm.

Activity logs can help you schedule your day more efficiently. The fewer times you change tasks, the more efficient your work flow will become. Perhaps your log shows you that you check your email six or seven times a day (I know my log shows that). It is far more efficient if you read and respond to email in larger blocks than if you break off from whatever task you are working on to check every hour or so.

Knowing this, I now clear my mail of junk when I get up in the morning (Literally. I spend ten minutes in the morning clicking delete without reading anything). I then clear out work-related emails during my office hour. If necessary, I can extend that block, but usually an hour is plenty of time. Later, I might check my mail to look for urgent student messages, but I generally just ignore it until just before bed. Then I go through the delete process again, deal with any pressing work issues and answer any pressing personal emails. This three or four times a day process is far more efficient than when I left my mail open all day long and checked or cleared it the moment new messages arrived.

An additional benefit to using an activity log is that it may help you find those times in the day when you have more or less energy. Knowing the circadian rhythms of your body (the cycle of highs and lows in your energy levels throughout a day) can help you better plan your day to be more effective. If you know you don't really get going in the day until after 9 am, you likely don't want to schedule high-powered meetings or physical activities at 8 am.

I learned many years ago that I am a "middle of the day" person. It takes me a bit in the morning to get going and I generally can't stay up late while remaining productive. As such, I have found that scheduling my office hour in the morning and any face to face classes in the early evening is the most productive schedule for me. I've maintained that schedule for more than seven years now.

Once you've assessed the results of your activity logs, it's time to begin prioritizing your day.

Setting Priorities

Setting priorities, while one of the key elements of solid time management, can be one of the hardest tasks to complete. I think this is especially true for the consensual slave since his or her priorities must include the priorities of the owner as well as personal priorities. Brian Tracy (2003), a leading authority on personal and business success, describes six ideas to use when setting priorities.

1. Be clear about your goals and objectives. Having a clear picture of your goal will help you set priorities which move you toward those goals. Ensure that as you set your goals and objectives you do so with a clear idea of how the outcome will affect your life, career, or relationships. Doing so will help you stay on track to gain those things which are of value to you.

2. Use a long-term perspective when you prioritize so you can choose to work on those things which will have the greatest impact on your future. Remember to include all areas of your life when looking at the long-term goals. Don't forget your health in favor of focusing on your career. Don't let your relationships suffer in favor of other priorities.

3. Commit to improving the areas of your life which are most important to you. Take time to learn to be better at what you feel is important. If you want to be a better servant, learn new skills. If you want to be a better parent, learn to be a better parent. Whatever your passions, whatever will improve your life while taking you closer to your overall goals, make that a priority.

4. Give yourself enough time to do things right the first time. Having to redo tasks not only takes more time, it will affect your confidence in yourself and your skills. Don't rush when planning would have made rushing unnecessary.

5. Keep in mind that the overall amount of time you spend working toward your goals is not nearly as important as the time you spend working on high-priority tasks. If the task is high-priority, it should be a task which will advance you toward your goal. Spending eight hours a day at work, but spending only five hours on high-priority tasks will not advance you toward your goals the way spending eight hours on high-priority tasks will. The outcome may be the same, but isn't it far more satisfying to reach a goal ahead of schedule than to have to scramble to meet deadline?

6. Your ability to make wise choices is what will make setting priorities

work. Choosing to spend a day on low-priority tasks may be initially satisfying, but the consequences of time lost for high-priority tasks may be enormous. Learning to delay gratification and accept responsibility for the choices you make will help you learn to prioritize effectively.

While Tracy's ideas are certainly cogent to setting priorities, sometimes a more practical approach is helpful to get started. Go back to your activity logs and be sure you have classified the tasks by priority. Once you've done so, you can begin using the "three-list method" of defining priorities advocated by Donald Martin (1991), author of *How to Be a Successful Student*.

Start with a weekly calendar. Include all priority activities for the week on this calendar. In my case, I would include my office hours (times when I must be in a particular place) and my exercise times. These are the only currently completely structured parts of my day. Once you have your "must be here" times scheduled, fill in your other priorities where they fit your schedule. Perhaps you have a regular appointment to get your nails done, or maybe there are certain television shows you simply can't miss. Fill in the week with those tasks which will move you forward toward your goals. Remember to be flexible when necessary. Perhaps I planned (as I did this morning) to write for a few hours after my office hour, but something came up which needed my immediate attention. I can shift from writing to the other task because I know being flexible will mean I have time for both tasks.

Keep a daily "Things to Do" list. I have done this for years because I have Swiss cheese memory. If I don't write it down, it likely won't get done. The other advantage of making a daily list is that you know when you have finished your high-priority tasks and can spend time on lower-priority, but possibly more fun, tasks. And, if you're anything like me, there's definitely pleasure to be gained from checking items off a list.

Keeping a things to do list will help you find areas of your life which are overwhelming you. If you list a task each day, but each day you're unable to complete that task, you can review the rest of the list and adjust priorities. Reviewing your list is key to maintaining relevant priorities. If you spend time on low-value tasks while high-value tasks go unfinished, your list will show you this.

Keeping a long-term list of goals and tasks is also helpful in keeping yourself on task and moving forward. Make a list of long term goals. Include tasks necessary to complete your goals and prioritize them in the weekly calendar and daily task list.

Setting priorities can be difficult, but when done right, doing so will help you work more efficiently and help you find ways to fit more into your day. Such a skill is especially helpful for the consensual slave who is often faced with balancing their own priorities with those of their owner. Learn to prioritize and you will make yourself even more valuable to your owner.

Using Action Plans

Once you've learned to effectively prioritize your daily, weekly, and monthly tasks, you'll find that using action plans to reach short-term and long-term goals will help you be more successful. An action plan is nothing more complicated than a prioritized list of tasks necessary to accomplish a specified goal. Action plans can help you stay organized while completing complicated tasks.

For example, your owner tells you he is going on a business trip. Your task is to ensure everything is packed and ready for him to leave on time. Your action plan would include all tasks necessary to get him packed and ready. Maybe you need to take his suits to the cleaner, pick up travel information for the city he's traveling to, and arrange for transportation to the airport. Make a list with all accompanying tasks for each of those necessary tasks and then prioritize. I would likely take the suits to the cleaners first, since that may take a day or two. Then I would arrange for the transportation to ensure it was available at the right time. Finally, I would collect information on the city he is traveling to and include a packet of information in his briefcase with restaurants, drug stores, and points of interest near his hotel should he choose to visit anything or need anything while he was gone. I would also make a list of all necessary garments and toiletries to be packed for the trip after talking with him to determine what activities he might engage in and checking weather forecasts for the city he is headed to. That list would not only be used to pack his luggage, but would be included with the city information so he would know what he had at his disposal.

Preparing an owner for a trip can be stressful simply because there are often a hundred small details that you might not think of unless you take time to plan. Using an action plan will keep you focused and help you find areas you didn't consider so your owner doesn't arrive at his location only to find he is lacking something he really needed.

Action plans can be prepared in advance and reused for similar tasks. If your owner travels a lot, make a travel action plan and update it with specifics for each location he or she travels to. If you need to produce a work place document each month, make an action plan with the basic steps necessary to make the document and update it each month with specifics. If you know someone who already has an action plan for something you're going to need to do, use it! Don't reinvent the wheel. I recommend Elegant's[38] article on travel preparations for your master found in the February 2006 *Simply Service*[39] as a great action plan to work with and adapt to your own needs.

Overcoming Procrastination

The final bar to being an efficient and effective servant (or salesperson, or teacher or mom) is procrastination. Procrastination is the putting off of high-value tasks in favor of low-value tasks. Usually, I know when I'm procrastinating and my motivation toward the goal I'm putting off is what will either prolong or end the procrastination. For example, I put off writing this chapter of the book until nearly all the other chapters were complete because the relationship stuff is more interesting most of the time. It was only when I realized the value in this chapter to the book as a whole that I stopped putting it off and began writing it.

---

[38] Elegant began her leather journey in Dallas, Texas and has been an active part of the Atlanta community since moving in 2001. She does not like being identified with a single label, as her identity is a blending of her life. She is slave to Master Archer, mother to two pre-teens, PTA volunteer, leather crafter, bootblack, Group Event Coordinator for 1763 and co-owner of Fantasies In Leather. Elegant is a member of The Tribe, CAPE, National Leather Association International, NLA-Dallas, MAST-Atlanta, Publicity and Fundraising Chair for SouthEast LeatherFest and the creator of the Atlanta Fetish Flea Market. Elegant had the honor of being selected as Southeast Bootblack 2005 at Together In Leather and 1st Runner-Up at International Community Bootblack 2005.

[39] This issue is available here through the Simply Service Yahoo Group. You can join it here: http://groups.yahoo.com/group/SimplyService/

Servants will procrastinate for many reasons. Sometimes we put off onerous tasks in favor of doing fun tasks. Sometimes we feel overwhelmed by our daily list and procrastinate as a stress response. We may even fear success or failure and so we put off working on tasks which will bring us to one or the other. And then there are the perfectionists (like me), who feel they cannot begin a task until all the conditions are exactly right. Whatever your reason for procrastinating, there are ways to combat this usually destructive behavior pattern.

First, recognize that you are procrastinating (Overcoming procrastination, 2007). Use your daily task lists and action plans to find areas of your priorities which are being neglected. Then do something about it. If you find you are avoiding working on a project, get started. If there are chores you hold off on, do them first. Break the pattern of procrastination by first admitting there is a pattern.

Next, figure out why you're procrastinating (Overcoming procrastination, 2007). Look closely at your priorities and examine those you are avoiding. Be honest with yourself here. Are you avoiding the project because you don't feel prepared to start it? Are you putting off cleaning the bathroom because you're overwhelmed by how messy it has become? Whatever the reason, your next task is to find ways to get past the reason and into the task.

Finally, get over it (Overcoming procrastination, 2007). If you are avoiding something because you don't want to do it, but you can't delegate the task to someone else, find a way to motivate yourself. Maybe you really want a pedicure. Make that your reward for finishing the project you've been putting off. Perhaps you'd like new towels. Get them as a reward for cleaning the bathroom regularly for a month. Whatever motivations will work for you, use them. As a consensual slave, we have the added motivation of our owners. If their pleasure is motivation for you, use it. If their displeasure over your procrastination is motivating, use that as well. Whatever you need to get going, use it.

Getting organized and learning to manage your time will help you be a better servant. For me, I know that when I am organized and working at peak efficiency, the little surprises which seem to crop up in my life regularly are far less likely to throw me out of whack. Remember that your owner chose you as their servant because they believed you could handle the responsibility. Keeping yourself organized will help you meet that expectation.

(2007). Action plans: Small scale planning. Retrieved November 2, 2007, from Mind Tools Web site: http://www.mindtools.com/pages/article/neHTE_04.htm

(2007). Activity logs: Finding out how you really spend your time. Retrieved November 2, 2007, from Mind Tools Web site: http://www.mindtools.com/pages/article/newHTE_03.htm

Martin, D (1991). How to manage time and set priorities. Retrieved November 6, 2007, from College of Marin Web site: http://www.marin.cc.ca.us/~don/Study/5time.html

(2007). Overcoming procrastination: Manage your time. Get it all done.. Retrieved November 2, 2007, from Mind Tools Web site: http://www.mindtools.com/pages/article/newHTE_96.htm

Tracy, B (2001). Setting Priorities. Retrieved November 6, 2007, from Time Management Tools Web site: http://www.time-management-tools.com/articles/setting-priorities.htm

Separations and Long Distance Relationships

Just as power exchange relationships mirror vanilla relationships in other areas, so too do they mirror the problems of long-distance relationships or separations. Being separated from those we love is never easy. When you are living as a consensual slave, separation can be even more difficult because so much of how we live is tied to caring for our owners.

I want to offer you some suggestions for dealing with separations and long-distance relationships. These are tactics I have used during both types of relationships and I hope they will help you as they have helped me.

First, please understand that I do not now, nor have I ever, engaged in an Internet-only relationship. I don't pretend to understand them, though of course I applaud your dedication to such a relationship. I have dealt with a long-distance relationship which developed when the man I served moved to another state and I have dealt with extended separations when the man I now serve is called away by his work. I recognize that these situations are completely different than Internet-only or phone-only relationships, and as such I may not have any specific suggestions for you. However, I believe most long-distance relationships share enough in common that my approaches should help you as well.

Communication

First, and I know you're tired of hearing it, but it's necessary, clear, consistent and regular communication is imperative to the success of long-distance relationships. If you don't see each other regularly, you have to talk to each other. And while I understand that there is generally more cost involved with phone communication verses Internet communication, the lack of tone present in Internet communication makes it a less reliable form of clear communication. That being said, if Internet (i.e. email, chat and instant message) communication is all you have access to, use it and use it regularly.

Not only is it important to clearly communicate the relationship tasks and ideas, regular communication helps keep the members of a long-distance relationship connected. Isolation and distance are very real and common feelings among partners who are physically separated. Talking, emailing and instant messaging regularly will help you stay connected and help to keep you from facing the miscommunication which invariably arise over distance.

If you're engaged in a long-distance relationship as a consensual slave you know how silence from your owner can be frightening and aggravating at the same time. When I served a man who moved several states away and weeks would go by with no contact, I would begin to go through a cycle of anger and fear that was quite destructive to both my emotional health and the relationship as a whole. More consistent communication on his part would have helped to maintain the health of our relationship.

Now, I do have to caution you to consider the circumstances behind the silences that sometimes arise in long-distance relationships. Because I know what the man I now serve does when he's away, gaps in communication are expected and easily dealt with because he has always reconnected as soon as he was able. Keeping lines of communication open and sharing information about the means, method and frequency of communication will help you stay balanced and keep you connected with your partner.

Staying Connected

If the separation is planned, before you separate, make plans with your owner to develop ways to stay connected and in your station while you're apart. Daily tasks, communication expectations, and maintenance of protocol will help you both maintain your station and remain connected to each other.

There was a time when I took photographs of the clothing I would wear for a week and sent them to the man I was in service to. I did this every week on Sunday so he could approve or deny the outfits and know what I was wearing any given day. I also kept a detailed online calendar which I sent to him each morning so he'd know where I was and what I was doing. These tasks helped me maintain my station and allowed me to serve him from a distance.

When the man I now serve left for his job the last time, I started writing letters from the day he left. I mailed the letters each day. The letters served several purposes for me. First, they kept me connected to him. All the silly things I would normally have told him on the phone, I wrote in the letters (and often later told him on the phone too...he told me when he came home that he'd laugh reading the letters because he already knew what was in them). Second, writing that letter was a daily task I completed before bed. It kept me focused on him each day. And third, taking the letter to the mailbox, a trip that was often out of the way of my most efficient daily commute, was another way to connect to him. I would end the day by writing the letter and start the day by mailing it. The letters made me keep track of things like how many stamps I had, whether I needed to print labels and whatnot, so there was very little time while he was away that he wasn't on my mind.

Whatever works for you to stay connected, do it. I enjoyed writing the letters and would definitely do it again should he need to go away again. But if you don't like to write, find something else you can do to stay connected. Maybe you call at a particular time, or keep up your daily chores from when your owner was closer. Whatever it is you do, share it with your owner. Chances are, they are looking for ways to stay connected too (remember that human element?) and they might enjoy your suggestions. I know the sweetest thing the owner said to me about our separation was, "Anytime I needed you, you were just a letter away."

Reconnecting in Person

When that wonderful time comes that you and your owner will be together again, make sure you plan some readjustment time. Separation from your owner and the day to day interactions on an owner/servant level may make the reconnection awkward. If you're prepared for it, getting past the awkwardness and finding your way back to your accustomed place will be much easier.

I know a couple who, due to work obligations, have spent a significant portion of their relationship apart from each other. Each time they get close to a reunion, the servant becomes agitated and often angry with the owner. It is a pattern that has been repeated over the span of years and which the owner is now ready to handle. He does what he can to mitigate the anger and fear and when they are physically together again, he is ruthless in his application of protocol. Experience has taught them that this is the only way to reconnect and return to what is normally a happy and healthy power exchange relationship.

Whatever you and your owner agree upon for your reconnection, negotiate some time for it to happen. Even if you're so happy to see them you burst into tears in a parking lot when they surprise you by coming home early, you may find hidden landmines that only time will relieve. If you take time and keep communicating, you'll find what works for your relationship and your reconnections will become part of the routine of your relationship.

I know of many successful long-distance power exchange relationships. I know of many who have attempted such relationships only to find they didn't work out. Being separated from the one you serve is stressful. You have to remain true to the relationship without your owner's immediate input. If you aren't self-motivated, you'll likely find long-distance relationships difficult. I recommend taking time to carefully negotiate your duties and tasks prior to a separation so you know what to expect and can make adjustments without distance to complicate things. And last but not least, keep talking to each other while you're separated. Communicate when and how you can and you'll find the distance will shrink and your relationship will remain on an even keel until your reunion.

Just as consensual slavery relationships are not for everyone, so too are long-distance relationships only for the stout of heart. Mixing the two together makes both issues even more difficult but also all that much more rewarding when you are successful. Work hard at your relationship and the distance will fade.

The Great Balancing Act

Wouldn't it be wonderful if we didn't need to compartmentalize our lives? If power exchange relationships weren't taboo in mainstream society and we didn't need to separate our leather lives from our vanilla lives? Unfortunately such usually isn't the case. Our bosses may not think collars fit into the corporate dress code and likely wouldn't want us taking the day off because our owners want to leave us in bondage for the day. And so begins the great balancing act. How do consensual slaves balance their vanilla responsibilities with their service responsibilities?

The best place to start the balancing act is in the negotiation stage of your relationship. Be open and honest with your owner about your vanilla responsibilities. Do you have a demanding career? Are there children in the family who fall under your care? Are your parents ill? Any vanilla responsibilities which will require significant time and attention will need to be disclosed if you and your owner are going to be able to develop a plan to help you meet those obligations.

I was very clear when I negotiated my current power exchange relationship that my job can be very stressful at times and especially at the break in semesters. Four times a year I have to grade final papers and prepare for new classes to begin. At those times, my vanilla responsibilities must take precedence as they are what supports me and my lifestyle.

Conversely, the owner has been frank with me regarding his vanilla responsibilities. I know that his job often calls him away with little or no notice. I agreed to work with that stipulation in our relationship as part of our negotiation, just as he agreed to understand my need for more personal time when my semesters change.

When you sit down to assess your needs (as I recommend you do prior to negotiating your power exchange relationship) make sure you include the need to meet your vanilla responsibilities in that list. I've given up part-time jobs in the past because I couldn't find a healthy balance between the responsibilities of those jobs and the need to care for the man I was in service to at the time. You may find you need to do something similar to maintain balance in your life.

If you haven't already done so, read the chapter on Organization and Time Management in this book. Learning to prioritize will help immensely as you attempt this balancing of vanilla and leather responsibilities. That chapter will also help you develop and use action plans and schedules. Those two tools will make an enormous difference in your ability to balance your priorities.

If you have a schedule in which your vanilla priorities and service priorities are given appropriate time to meet your goals, you'll be far more successful than if you simply try to wing it. Schedules help keep you focused on the daily tasks, which in turn will keep you focused on your goals.

The man I am in service to now knows that I must be in my office for an hour each day. He also knows that there will be times when I have face to face classes which will require my presence. By sharing my schedule with him, I have shared my availability for his priorities. He knows that Tuesday through Friday I am not available to him from 8-9 am because I'm in my office. He can then make adjustments to his need for me to perform tasks since those office hours are a negotiated priority for our relationship. As a matter of fact, when the semester changed and I was able to change my office hours, I consulted the owner and he suggested the time when I have now scheduled them.

If you are self-motivated, strict schedules may not be necessary to keep you focused. If, however, you find you do not focus on necessary tasks without direction, a more structured schedule may help with your focus. Start with a schedule containing larger blocks and move to one with more narrow task times if you find you aren't able to meet your obligations with the looser version.

So what happens when your schedule is blown to pieces by that unexpected event? How do you handle surprises and their affect on your balance? As I noted in the humanity chapter, both servants and owners are both human first and either servant or owner after. That being the case, sometimes the best laid plans will be wrecked. You must learn to be flexible if you want to stay balanced.

I get phone calls throughout the day from the owner. He needs me to run an errand or add something to a website, or research something for a client. But what if I was doing something else? Something that is on my schedule even? Usually, my schedule is flexible enough for me to shift gears, take care of his priority, and get back to mine later. But I know my schedule isn't the norm.

The key here is communication. The man I serve knows he can call at any hour and I will be able to take care of things for him within an hour of his call. He knows this because I have shared my schedule with him. If you are clear in your communication with your owner regarding your availability, you'll know that should he or she need you outside a regularly available time, it's likely an emergency.

Flexibility is key to making nearly any relationship work. My boss often comes to me, hat in hand, and asks if I'm willing to take on another class or pick up a class no one else wants to teach. She does this because past experience has taught her that I generally will say yes, because I'm flexible and willing to do what the department needs for our students. The same is true of my power exchange relationships. Sure, I get annoyed when I'm writing and the phone rings. If there's something that has to be done right away, I sigh and put the keyboard aside and get to work. When I finish the new priority, I go back to my own. If you're willing and able to be flexible in your handling of surprises, you'll be happier and less stressed on the whole.

There may, however, come a time when you have to tell your owner "no." I know how hard it is for servants to say "no" in general and how it is nearly impossible to say no to those we serve. The reality is, however, that sometimes we must do exactly that.

Approach the need to say no as you would any other communication with your owner. Use diplomacy and be clear about the reasons for needing to say no. Being open about the cause of your inability to meet a request from you owner will help you both. Just saying no may cause conflict between you and your owner. Offering reasons for the no gives the owner the information necessary for them to understand you aren't just being arbitrary.

If, for example, the man I serve told me I needed to stay home this Thanksgiving, I would have to say no. I would go to him and explain that I have already promised my mother that I would come home this year and she has made plans which include me. At this point, it would be up to him to decided if my vanilla priority (which was clearly negotiated at the beginning of the relationship) outweighed any service priority which prompted his request that I remain in North Carolina for the holiday. Giving him the explanation would give him enough information to make an informed decision. This is, of course, not something he would do because I have kept him informed of my holiday plans from the first moment I considered a trip to my parents' home, but it serves as a good example.

The key to keeping up the balancing act is communicating with your owner. I would hope you have chosen to serve someone who would understand and agree to the negotiation of your vanilla priorities. Remember that you can, and should, keep your owner informed when you feel overwhelmed. Doing so gives them the opportunity to lift burdens from you or help you cull the extraneous things from your life. You trust this person with your body, mind and soul, don't handicap them by keeping information from them. Set your priorities, stay flexible and have fun. We choose this life and it chooses us. You'll find ways to stay balanced.

Wrapping it All Up

We've come to the end of this journey. The following chapters will share the last bits of my advice for creating and living a successful consensual slavery relationship. If you've come this far, I hope you will find value in these final thoughts.

Baring Your Soul

One of the scariest parts of being a consensual slave is opening up your soul to your owner and letting them into all the hidden corners where your worst fears hide. Doing so, however, will free you from controlling behaviors and open up the relationship to levels you might not have believed were possible.

The man I serve said something to me a week or so ago and it has reverberated through my brain ever since. He said he wanted, demanded even, "general power of attorney over my soul." He wanted no secrets, no withheld information between us. In short, he wanted everything I am and have hidden away from everyone else in my life up to now opened up and aired out to him.

To be honest, the idea terrifies me, and always has. There are parts of me I don't share with anyone.

- The destructive voices that tell me I'm worthless and unfit to belong to anyone.

- The cold-hearted bitch who comes out when I've been hurt by those I trusted.

- The hysterical little girl who still wonders what happened to the daddy she loved.

All those horrible things that I keep inside, he wants to see and hear about. And I will do it, because it is his right as the owner to demand every piece of me.

Eliminating Controlling Behavior

When your owner says I want to know everything, how do you handle that request? Do you mouth the correct response, all the while internally blocking off areas of yourself you won't share? Or do you take the sledge hammer to the walls you've already built and fire the contractors waiting in the wings to build new ones? Your approach to this request will have a profound affect on your power exchange relationship in the long run.

I've always had trouble asking for what I want or need. It started long before I ever engaged in a power exchange relationship and it stems, in part, from the many "nos" I got when I said I needed something in the past. Because I expect the answer to my request to be "no" I will often evaluate the importance of my request and either hold it or discard it based on my own perception of importance. It took an epiphany from my good friend Rick to show me that this habit of making judgment calls about my needs and desires was usurping the owner's power to grant or deny said needs and desires. If I don't present my needs and desires to the owner, I have made the decision for him, rather than giving him the necessary information for him to decide for himself what he would give his property.

Believe me when I say I understand your objections right now. "I serve someone who has a high-powered job and doesn't have time to deal with my daily wants and desires." or "I just don't want to bother her after a long day at work. She has enough on her mind." I've said those very things to myself time and time again and never even recognized the controlling behavior inherent in those statements. Better to open up, in an appropriate manner, and give your owner the right to decide rather than deciding for them.

If you serve someone with a high-powered or high-stress job, perhaps you need to devise a non-intrusive method of sharing your soul with them. Maybe you can keep a journal that they can read when they have time. Perhaps you can set aside an hour a week in which to share your thoughts, desires and needs. Whatever the solution, use it. Don't skimp on your journal when you know they are more stressed than usual. They'll notice and you'll be engaged in controlling behavior again. Trust that you've chosen the right person to serve and they will do everything in their power to care for and protect you. In short, give them "general power of attorney over your soul."

Rewards of Baring Your Soul

Once you've stopped controlling your owner by withholding information, you'll find that you will build trust in the relationship on both sides. Your owner will trust you to share everything with them and you will learn to trust that sharing things with them will result in positive outcomes for you. That is not to say that sharing every desire with your owner will result in them granting each one. It does mean that sharing everything about yourself with your owner will result in them being able to make informed decisions for you which will protect and care for you. The manner in which they protect and care for you may not be the one you would have chosen for yourself, but it will be done.

Fully opening yourself to your owner in this manner will also demonstrate your submission to their will. Withholding information, even if you believe it is in the best interest of your owner, is defiance. Defiance is contrary to submission and service. If you would be a consensual slave, you must be willing to submit to the whims, desires, and needs of your owner. One of those needs, unless otherwise negotiated, is likely to be the need to be kept informed of your thoughts, actions, and needs. Giving up control like this isn't easy but it does carry the reward of being better able to demonstrate your submission to your owner.

Once the trust is built between you and your owner because you are not withholding anything from them, you'll find that you will connect to them on a deeper level than before you completely submitted to them. There are few things as lovely as kneeling at the feet of your owner and knowing you have no secrets. He or she knows every ugly detail of your life and your spirit and they still want, even demand, your service. Reaching that point can be supremely fulfilling to a servant, especially since the journey to that place is incredibly difficult.

Getting Your Owner to Open Up Too

Another frustrating aspect of the baring of your soul is that you likely won't receive the same opening and sharing from your owner. They may choose to remain closed to you in ways they will not accept from you. If such is the case, you will have to abide by their desires. The man I serve rarely shares of himself without my questions, but he doesn't mind the questions. He has asked only that I don't ask others about him, rather that I go to him and ask the questions I have. I think that's a fair request and have always abided by it (even before he spoke it to me, having seen the negative affects of another servant asking about him rather than asking of him). If it is appropriate in your power exchange relationship, ask questions that delve into your owner's soul the way he or she will delve into yours. It is as important to know about their hopes and dreams as it is to know how they take their coffee. Since most dominants I've come in contact with are miserly about sharing of themselves, the only way to learn is to ask.

Of course, that opens another door into my soul for him to wander through. I've often wandered through relationships with the idea that unless the owner shared something with me, I didn't really need to know it. I found out the hard and painful way, that such is not always the case. Opening up and asking about his past, his present and his future is not easy for me, but I have found it to be necessary because I serve him better when I now what's going on. Just recently I swallowed back the pain an answer might cause and asked the question. I didn't get an answer, yet, but I did ask and that is what is important. Learning to ask the owner to open up is sometimes just as difficult as learning to open yourself to them. Find the appropriate means and methods and keep the communication flowing so neither of you is blindsided by something.

Why Is It So Hard

The best servants are self-sufficient men and women who are successful in their own right and don't need anyone to make them feel successful. It is a choice to submit to another and that choice is often seemingly contrary to every action which lead to their success in the first place. I've been on my own for many years. After a divorce, I have only lived in the same home with the man I served once, and then for less than a year. I hold a master's degree, which I earned before I came to the leather community. I am successful and self-sufficient. Letting go of my control over my life, my heart and my soul has been one of the hardest things I've ever done in my life. My trust issues with men have made it even harder to trust that opening up to the owner will result in anything other than my complete destruction. But I have done it and I have benefited from having trusted and opened up. It hasn't all been roses and kittens. There have been times of great pain to accompany the moments of exquisite pleasure. And they have each been tools to bring me to where I am now.

Your journey will likely be both similar and entirely different from mine. I can only offer what I have learned and hope you'll find some nugget of similarity to apply to your own path. Being a consensual slave is anything but easy, but it is also the single most fulfilling thing I've ever done in my life. I hope you will feel the same when your path has been laid out and followed.

Rewards of Service

So you've made it through all the practical chapters of this book and you're still with me. Thank you for that. There's nothing worse than knowing you wrote something that made someone want to throw the book across the room when they finished reading it. The question is, "Now what?" Or better yet, "Why would I put myself through all of that to become a consensual slave?" Truthfully, I can't answer that question for you, and I would hope after reading everything I've written, you really wouldn't want me to. Instead I can help you understand some of the phenomenal rewards of being a consensual slave.

Intrinsic Rewards

As noted in earlier chapters, servants should strive to find some intrinsic motivations for service to relieve their owners from the necessity of acknowledging every action or service. The added benefit to finding intrinsic motivation is the discovery of intrinsic rewards to service. Perhaps you find satisfaction in a job well done. Or maybe there is pleasure in a well-run home. Or do you simply glow with the knowledge that your owner is better able to achieve his or her goals because your service has freed them of tasks which might otherwise hinder their progress?

Whatever the specifics of your intrinsic rewards, know that they are satisfying in and of themselves. I know that the sight of his face early in the morning, harried though it was because he was running late, was wonderful because I was able to hand him the work he gave me the previous night and know he had one less thing on his plate this week. He thanked me, kissed and hugged me on the run, but honestly it was my internal reward of giving him the several hours of rest I knew he needed by taking the task and completing it for him that was most satisfying.

Find those things inside yourself that make you smile when you pour his coffee or brush her hair. Those are your intrinsic rewards. Cherish them and know that no matter what else, your heart swells with happiness when you serve those you love and love those you serve.

Extrinsic Rewards

There are, of course, external rewards for our service. Sometimes these rewards are what makes a week or a month's worth of hard work worth the effort. Sometimes they are just icing on the cake. Regardless of our status as servants, receiving extrinsic rewards for our service can be wonderful.

One of the protocols from a prior power exchange relationship I was engaged in was "Wants and desires will be met upon positive performance of duties and tasks." Having our desires granted can be a rare treat for the average consensual slave. But when we perform our service in ways that meet and/or exceed the expectations of our owners, we are far more likely to have our desires granted than should we perform below their expectations. Perhaps your owner will grant you something you've requested. Maybe they will arrange something as a surprise. Whatever it is, knowing you're being rewarded for your service makes the gift all that much more special.

If you're anything like me, the pride and appreciation received from the owner when a job is well done can erase any irritation doing the task might have raised. As I worked on the task given to me one evening, I was slightly irritated because I had wanted to complete this chapter before bed. However, the appreciation he offered the following morning more than made up for the necessity of putting off this chapter until later. I also know he's proud that he can give me a task and it will be done at his standard without the need for minute checks. I called when I had questions, wrote notes when there were explanations and left the finished product where he would find it even if I wasn't available to hand it over. I know that my attention to detail makes him proud to own me. That kind of reward means a lot to me, more so even than having desires granted, because it speaks directly to why he chooses to accept my service.

When your owner praises you and offers his or her appreciation, accept it with grace. I know it can be hard to accept appreciation for things we feel are our responsibility anyway, but accepting anything offered to us with grace is the mark of a well-trained servant. Thank them for their gift and offer any other relationship-appropriate connections. I got a hug and a kiss this morning. I'm a happy girl today.

If you and your owner go to leather events, you're likely to observe other servants and owners. Watch how other dominants look at and talk with your owner. Are they deferential? Are they inquisitive of the training you've received? Are they, perhaps, just a little envious of your owner and his or her property? If so, you've just stumbled onto another wonderful extrinsic reward.

If you are an accomplished servant, other dominants and owners will esteem your owner because they see how you do your job. They may ask your owner what their training process is, or ask you to mentor their own property in order to develop the kind of servant you demonstrate yourself to be. This esteem can be both extremely fulfilling to a servant and equally annoying. Being asked to mentor the smart ass masochist currently standing in the middle of the dungeon screaming, "look at me!" can be frustrating. Knowing that your owner receives the majority of the credit for your hard work in becoming the accomplished servant you are can be deflating to your ego. However, know that there is a certain amount of pride for you in being owned by someone other dominants look up to. And if they look up to him or her because of you, you have performed another service for your owner. You have made them appear as competent as you know they are in ownership. You wouldn't belong to just any schlub, would you? Take pride in the esteem others have for your owner and accept that esteem as a reward for your excellent service.

There are, of course, the leather contests you and your owner can compete in if you wish to earn even more extrinsic reward for your service. Regional, national and international master and slave competitions offer power exchange couples the opportunity to show the world their brand of power exchange and to receive rewards for doing it well. If you or your owner aspire to become community educators, a leather title contest might be just the ticket for you. I've met every regional and national master and slave title holder from my area for the past several years and I have learned from each couple and individual. The title contests are arduous, but if they are a goal for you and your owner, they are worth the effort.

For me, the rewards of service are balanced between the intrinsic and extrinsic with maybe a slight tilt toward the intrinsic. I serve because there is something in me that cries out to be of service. I am lucky enough to have found owners who have allowed that cry to be heard and put to good use.

Ultimately, each servant will need to define for themselves why they have chosen the path of the consensual slave. The journey is not an easy one and sometimes the rewards are few and far between. However, I know I have never been happier than when I am in service to an owner I love and care for and who loves and cares for me. I can only wish you the same luck in finding your way to this happiness.

Glossary

BDSM--Acronym for various permutations of Bondage/Discipline, Dominance/Submission, Sadism/Masochism. Used as a broad term to define the activities practiced in relationships of this type.

Bottom--the receiver of the activity during sadomasochistic play, often used interchangeably with masochist

Dominant--In a power exchange relationship, this is the partner who receives power from the submissive.

Leather Community--Broad term to identify the larger community of BDSM and including both hetero and homo sexual groups and members. By preference, the author of this text uses Leather Community in place of BDSM community because she feels the term is more broadly applicable.

Leather Sex or leathersex--the wide and nearly inexhaustible variety of sadomasochistic play engaged in by members of the Leather Community. Leather sex may or may not include intercourse.

Masochist--A sadomasochistic player who enjoys receiving pain. Often used interchangeably with bottom.

Master/Mistress--An honorific used to identify the dominant member of a power exchange relationship.

Owner--A gender non-specific honorific used to identify the dominant member of a power exchange relationship. This term is used in this text to identify the dominant members of total power exchange relationships.

Power exchange--The giving and receiving of power in a sadomasochistic relationship.

Sadist--A sadomasochistic player who enjoys inflicting pain. Often used interchangeably with top. This author's understanding of this term includes a differentiation between a sensual sadist and a sexual sadist. A sensual sadist enjoys (is sexually aroused) giving pain to those who enjoy receiving it. A sexual sadist is aroused by giving pain to those who do not enjoy it but suffer for them consensually.

Sadomasochistic play--Any of the variety of activities engaged in by members of the Leather Community, often involving the giving and receiving of pain.

Safeword--An arbitrary word agreed upon by sadomasochistic players that will end play.

Scene--A sadomasochistic play term denoting a specified time for participants to engage in a negotiated sharing of activities.

Servant--A gender non-specific term used to identify the submissive member of a power exchange relationship. This term is used in this text to identify the submissive members of total power exchange relationships.

Slave--A gender non-specific term used to identify the submissive member of a power exchange relationship. This term is used in this text to identify the submissive members of total power exchange relationships. Often this term carries weightier connotations than servant, but can be used interchangeably.

Submissive--A gender non-specific term used to identify the submissive member of a power exchange relationship.

Switch--A person in the Leather Community who alternately identifies as both top and bottom or both master and slave.

Top--The giver of an action in sadomasochistic play, often used interchangeably with sadist.

Vanilla--A term used to differentiate between the activities, preferences and lifestyle choices made by mainstream society and those made by members of the Leather Community. Vanilla refers to the choices and mindsets of the mainstream society.

Watersports--A particular sadomasochistic play involving urine.

Index

5070541R0

Made in the USA
Lexington, KY
31 March 2010